DOING *Your* BUSINESS RESEARCH PROJECT

SAGE was founded in 1965 by Sara Miller McCune to support the dissemination of usable knowledge by publishing innovative and high-quality research and teaching content. Today, we publish more than 750 journals, including those of more than 300 learned societies, more than 800 new books per year, and a growing range of library products including archives, data, case studies, reports, conference highlights, and video. SAGE remains majority-owned by our founder, and on her passing will become owned by a charitable trust that secures our continued independence.

Los Angeles | London | Washington DC | New Delhi | Singapore

John Beech

DOING *Your* BUSINESS
RESEARCH PROJECT

Los Angeles | London | New Delhi
Singapore | Washington DC

Los Angeles | London | New Delhi
Singapore | Washington DC

SAGE Publications Ltd
1 Oliver's Yard
55 City Road
London EC1Y 1SP

SAGE Publications Inc.
2455 Teller Road
Thousand Oaks, California 91320

SAGE Publications India Pvt Ltd
B 1/I 1 Mohan Cooperative Industrial Area
Mathura Road
New Delhi 110 044

SAGE Publications Asia-Pacific Pte Ltd
3 Church Street
#10-04 Samsung Hub
Singapore 049483

Editor: Kirsty Smy
Assistant editor: Nina Smith
Production editor: Sarah Cooke
Copyeditor: Gemma Marren
Proofreader: William Baginsky
Indexer: David Rudeforth
Marketing manager: Catherine Slinn
Cover design: Francis Kenney
Typeset by: C&M Digitals (P) Ltd, Chennai, India
Printed and bound by CPI Group (UK) Ltd,
Croydon, CR0 4YY

Library of Congress Control Number: 2014936835

British Library Cataloguing in Publication data

A catalogue record for this book is available from
the British Library

ISBN 978-1-84920-021-9
ISBN 978-1-84920-022-6 (pbk)

At SAGE we take sustainability seriously. Most of our products are printed in the UK using FSC papers and boards.
When we print overseas we ensure sustainable papers are used as measured by the Egmont grading system.
We undertake an annual audit to monitor our sustainability.

Contents

Contents

List of Tables

List of Figures

Preface

Let's face it – nobody ever met the prospect of doing an undergraduate business **project** with squeals of delight!

That's not to say that you won't be delighted when you finish it, both in the sense 'Thank goodness I've finished!', and in the sense 'Hey, I'm really proud of that!'. The aim of this book is to ease you towards those two particular pleasure zones, especially if your starting point is one of uncertainty, dread or downright fear.

Just as the business project is very different from any other assessment you have undertaken – for a start, you get to write the question, which is more of a hindrance than a help – this book recognises that it needs to be different from other textbooks too.

The key differences are:

- Because everybody's project is different in terms of its content, this book is partly a workbook, for you to customise by writing things in, so that it will help you with *your* project.
- You may well have some lectures to support you in doing your project, but the chances are that for most of the time you will be working on your own. The book has been written in a deliberately 'easy access' style, because it will be your companion in the wee small hours of the night as you are hunched over your laptop, bashing away with a lot of hesitation, unable to 'ask the lecturer afterwards'.
- To make it an easy read, I've adopted a style of writing that is more like the spoken word. It's rather less dry than you may be used to in a normal textbook, and it's not a style that you should copy in your project. But I think that one of the problems with normal textbooks is that they are *too* dry. While I'm serious all the time, that doesn't mean there won't be any moments of lighter relief – nothing exactly LMFAO you understand, an uncomfortable experience in any case I would imagine, and one that I wouldn't wish on you.

It's also different from most other books covering the same subject in another very significant way. It doesn't assume you are destined to get a First with the minimum of effort, just by being naturally gifted. It assumes you are no direct threat to Bill Gates or Richard Branson just yet, but that you are a pretty regular undergraduate student, reasonably intelligent (after all, you wouldn't have got into university if you weren't), and that you want the basics of how to complete a good, if not brilliant, project. It will certainly help you do a brilliant project if there is one inside you currently struggling to get out.

Project

A self-contained piece of work. Throughout this book the word is used in the specific context of an undergraduate research project.

Maybe you are dreading doing the project. What you have to do, and how you have to do it, may seem daunting. Perhaps you feel you don't actually have a project in you trying to escape. With the help of this book, you should be able to find that project, grow it into something a lot better than half decent, and hand in something which you can genuinely feel proud of. The project will probably be the longest thing you will ever write, so give it your best shot. This book will help you do exactly that.

Two key points to remember when doing your project:

Research

A systematic process for adding to the body of knowledge through an evidence-based approach.

- Learning to do **research** is very much about learning a particular way of thinking. Doing research is about questioning why or how something has happened or happens, working out a logical way of finding the answer, gathering evidence to support an answer in a systematic way, and finally coming to a logical conclusion – the only possible answer to your original question.
- Research is rarely dramatic or earth shattering, but is about adding to the body of knowledge in even a small way. You become the first person to know something for certain, which is in its own way satisfying. It doesn't necessarily happen overnight – the researchers who invented the transistor had been working at their research for quite a few years before making the major breakthrough.

The book has been developed from twenty years of experience of supervising and supporting students in writing undergraduate business projects, Masters business dissertations, and Doctoral theses, at De Montfort University and Coventry University, and also at the University of Applied Sciences, Kufstein, Austria, where I am a Visiting Professor, and the Russian International Olympic University in Sochi, where I am an International Professor. I have a debt of gratitude to the students I've supervised and taught, who have made me think more deeply about the best way to explain everything to do with research projects. Over the years there have been the Good, the Bad, and even the Ugly, but all of them have unknowingly contributed indirectly to this book. It is to them it is dedicated.

How to Use this Book

This book is very different from the kind of book you are used to. This should not be completely surprising, as the project is very different from the kind of coursework assessments that you are used to.

What you will be used to in a piece of assessment is being asked a question or set a task by your lecturer, for which you then, typically, have to prepare an essay or a report. Because everyone has been given the same piece of assessment, everyone will produce broadly similar essays or reports. The project is essentially different – most obviously because not only do you get to choose the **topic** of the project, you *have* to choose the topic.

As a result, while every project follows the general scheme of things in doing research, each project is highly individual in its content. Someone marking projects will obviously see both strong similarities in the format of every project and also the highly individual subject matter of each individual project.

This book aims to help all of you doing a project by taking you through the common **process**, while at the same time getting you to move forward in developing your own highly personal and individual content. Throughout the book there are write-in boxes where you can apply what you have been studying to your specific project. The boxes include reflective exercises to develop your understanding and practice of research skills, and write-in tasks which will form the basis of the design for your project.

I recommend that you first read through the book once from beginning to end before you start to create your project. Don't write anything into the boxes; leave this to the second working through the book. It does no harm to think about what you might want to write into the boxes, but don't actually write anything in, and don't let the boxes and exercises distract you from getting this first broad overview of what the book is about.

This will give you a good general overview of what you will need to do in order to get your project up and running. It will provide a basis for writing a project proposal if your university requires you to hand one in. It will raise lots of questions in your mind, which might worry you a little. Don't worry! This is perfectly normal, and is a situation that everyone who has ever done a project will have faced. What you need to do is then work in a systematic way, facing these troubling questions in a particular order.

Topic

The topic of your research project is the context (in particular, the industry sector and the business function, such as marketing or finance) in which it is embedded.

Process

A systematic series of actions carried out in a particular order to achieve an ultimate goal.

As you work your way through the book you will come across certain key words. The first time they appear, they will be printed in bold, and a box explaining them will be nearby. They are all printed together in the glossary, which begins on page 163.

So, once you have completed this first 'non-stop' run through the book, you should then begin to work your way through again from the beginning, chapter by chapter, doing the exercises and filling in the boxes as you go. This will establish the basis for doing your own project.

Once you are up and running, you can return to the book as a handbook at any time. To summarise:

- First read through – read all the way through; don't stop and do the exercises or fill in the boxes.
- Second read through – read through again, chapter by chapter; do stop and do the exercises or fill in the boxes; stop and reflect as you finish each chapter; aim to start each further chapter as a new work session.
- Downloadable copies of the various checklists and templates are available free from the SAGE website at study.sagepub.com/beech
- When you find it necessary, go back and dip in to specific chapters as 'revision', or 'read ahead' out of interest.

Enjoy!
John Beech

Key to Icons

These icons are used throughout the book. Make sure you are clear what they stand for.

 Stop and write in your personal answers now. You should be able to do this quickly.

 Stop and be prepared to do some work away from the book. This will involve some personal reflection, and you will need to spend some time thinking.

 This logo is used to draw attention to information that may not apply to every reader. You will need to think whether it applies to you.

 Keep coming back to this as you progress through the production of your project.

 Do one of the exercises at the back of the book designed to develop your research skills and competences.

 Recommended reading. I have been careful to recommend only books that are an accessible read, and which are relatively cheap (but try your university library first!).

Remember, wherever space has been left in a box you should write your response in. In this way you will customise this workbook towards your own individual project.

SECTION 1

What Is Research?

Section guide

Before you begin to construct your own project, you need to understand what research is, what the research project is all about, and how you can start to build a high-quality research project.

In this section you will work your way through to the answers to the following questions:

1. Why is the research project important to me?
2. What will I get out of it?
3. Why do I need to know about it in the first and second years when I only get to do it in the final year?
4. What is research all about?
5. What happens if it all starts to go pear shaped?
6. How will I be able to tell if my project is any good?
7. How relevant is this project to working in the real world?

Ready then? The great adventure begins here!

1

Introduction

Chapter objectives

By completing the work in this chapter, you should be able to:

- understand the basic nature of research
- appreciate the importance and significance of your research project to you
- relate the research you will do to research undertaken in the real business world
- see a rough outline of the road ahead of you.

Introduction

Of course it's tempting to start work on your project by opening a new Word file, called Project.docx, and typing away. To be honest, that's a bit like jumping into the driving seat of a car for the first time ever and expecting to start driving off on a long journey. It isn't going to work, and pretty rapidly you'd come to the conclusion that driving is an impossible skill to acquire. The normal way to learn to drive would begin with learning something about cars and how they are actually operated through their controls, and some basic roadcraft, all well away from the steering wheel.

In this chapter, you will learn the corresponding background information for writing your project, and start to acquire the skills and competences you will need.

If you are suffering from an almost overwhelming urge to dash off a questionnaire and rush out into the street with it, pressing it onto startled and unsuspecting passers-by, resist it! It's the equivalent of heading out onto the motorway on your first ever trip driving a car.

Why is the research project important to me?

The chances are that you bought this book because you have no choice over your business project – at most universities you have to do one to get your degree, or at least to get an Honours degree. Of course, business degrees at different universities have different regulations, and for this book to work for you at your university you will need to customise it. So the very first thing for you to do is answer the following straightforward questions. If you are not already sure of the answers, ask your tutor or, better still, check out the module descriptor from your university intranet (Blackboard, Moodle or whatever).

Is the business project compulsory in my degree programme?	YES / NO
Is it essential if I want to get an Honours degree?	YES / NO

Whenever you see the pencil in this book, it means you have to customise – this is what will produce your project for you.

If you answered 'Yes' to either or both questions, it's clear why you will want to pass the project. But is a 'pass' all that you are looking for?

To answer that question with any degree of seriousness, you will need to work out how much the marks for the project count towards your final degree classification. Here there is very great variety across the project modules in different degrees at different universities, so you will need to do some basic calculations to fill in the next part.

Does your final degree classification depend only on your final year marks? (If your answer is 'it depends because our mark is calculated in several different ways', you will need to work through the questions for each way of calculating it. I've assumed below, for simplicity, that your answer is 'yes'.)	YES / NO / IT DEPENDS
How many CATS points make up the full final year?	360
How many CATS points is the business project worth?	
What percentage of the CATS points for the final year's marks are down to the project? (Your last answer divided by 360 and then multiplied by 100.)	

Once you've reached that answer, it should be clear that in all probability the project carries significant weighting in determining your final degree classification. A good project is, for example, enough to pull your classification up to a 2:1 from a 2:2, but, on the other hand, a poor project is enough to drag a potential 2:2 down to a Third. So, it's pretty important, and, given that it's all still to play for, you have some power to improve your classification if you put the effort into it.

Regular modules don't have the same power of affecting your classification, so why is it that the project has this special status? It all comes down to why the project is in your degree programme.

When universities design their degree programmes, they have certain benchmarks, defined by a body called the Quality Assurance Agency for Higher Education, or QAA for short. They are not allowed to just bung any old thing into the syllabus – there are certain basics that must be there to justify the name of the degree, whether it be Business Studies, or Business Administration, or even other degrees with the word 'Management' in their name, such as Sports Management, Events Management or Tourism Management.

Degrees in business have the following requirements to meet included in the QAA Benchmark Statement for general business and management degrees:

> 3.9 Graduates should be able to demonstrate a range of cognitive and intellectual skills together with techniques specific to business and management. Graduates should also be able to demonstrate relevant personal and interpersonal skills. These include …
>
> – ability to conduct research into business and management issues, either individually or as part of a team for projects/dissertations/presentations. This requires familiarity with and an evaluative approach to a range of business **data**, sources of information and appropriate methodologies, and for such to inform the overall learning process
>
> – self-reflection and criticality including self-awareness, openness and sensitivity to diversity in terms of people, cultures, business and management issues. Also, the skills of learning to learn and developing a continuing appetite for learning; reflective, adaptive and collaborative learning.
>
> (Quality Assurance Agency for Higher Education, 2007)

Data

Systematically gathered bits of information. 'Data' is actually the plural of 'datum', but most people don't use the word 'datum' any more.

Most universities have retained the project, which complies with this benchmark, in a format that complied with earlier versions, which specifically required a demonstration that students were capable of conducting *sustained*, *independent* research (my emphasis).

It is the sustained and independent elements that make the project module so different from other modules. All your other modules operate within a standard timeframe of either a semester or an academic year. Although the project may officially take place within the confines of your final year, there will probably be either parts of earlier modules, or even entire modules, devoted to preparing you for it. In an ideal world you will have been thinking more and more about how you are going to set about your project before you reach your final year.

This may all seem a bit airy-fairy, but now is the time for a dose of hard reality: that is, the time to think about exactly how far away the dreaded hand-in date is. I know you are avoiding thinking about it, but you do need to seriously think about pacing yourself. The work you put into it is after all supposed to be sustained, and leaving it to the last minute is a sure-fire way of getting a bad mark.

When is the hand-in date? (The answer will be in your module descriptor. If you are currently in your second or even first year, you can, for the moment, work with your best guesstimate based on this year's hand-in date, but remember to update what you have written here when you hit your final year!)

What is the date today?

How many days are there from now until hand-in? (You can use a handy gizmo available at www.timeanddate.com/date/duration.html to do this calculation easily.)

It's very important to keep this ever-diminishing timeframe in mind. To help you do this, there is a natty countdown gizmo which you can personalise at www.timeanddate.com/countdown/create.

By the way, if you've just spent the last twenty minutes on timeanddate.com, seeing how long it is until Christmas, your cat's birthday or when the next leap year day is, you've discovered that very natural but not very helpful phenomenon known as 'displacement activity' – doing something which is an enjoyable way of avoiding doing something of a higher priority. To be honest, displacement activity isn't necessarily all bad. The problem is when it gets out of control. There's no harm in getting into the habit of taking a break from working on your project for five minutes every hour or so. In fact,

I would recommend it. Just make sure you don't spend fifty-five minutes on displacement activity and five minutes on your project. It's all a matter of the right balance.

Let's turn now to what's in it for you.

What will I get out of it?

The simple and obvious answer is that the project has the potential to get you a better degree classification. Isn't that enough?

Here are some other answers that may convince you to give the project your best shot.

Something to wow them with at a job interview

If you've got a clear idea of the business sector you want to go into when you graduate, and even have a specific company in mind, it may well serve you well to locate your project in that area. Come the interview, you will already have a thorough knowledge which you can impress the interview board with – take your project with you (providing it got a good mark!) and show them the data you gathered, the analysis you conducted and the conclusions you came to. I know of a number of cases where students have walked into their dream job on the back of a strong project which they showed at interview.

Probably the only book you'll ever write

You may find it hard to believe at this stage, but you will get an enormous buzz when you pick up your project after having it bound for handing in. A book! All your own work! It's something you will be proud enough of to give a copy to your parent(s) or guardian as a way of saying thank you for their support through your student days, and they will be immensely proud of you as a result.

A set of transferable micro-skills that will help you in the real world of work

As you will see as we progress through this book, in order to produce your project you will develop a good number of micro-skills related to doing research. In almost any job you will have to do some research, whether it is in developing a business plan or even a strategy, in assessing what your competitors are doing, or market research among your customers. All these micro-skills will be relevant, and by developing them during your project you will be enhancing your employability.

Remember that it's the micro-skills which will be useful in the real world – you are most unlikely ever to write something similar again, unless you go on to do a Masters degree. What you *will* be asked to write though are shorter, pithier reports in order to brief your boss on something. You will do this a lot better if you have the experience of an undergraduate project behind you.

A more critical way of thinking

This is arguably the most important benefit of doing your project. As you develop your skills of analysis and synthesis, you will begin to think more critically. You will be more critical in assessing 'facts' presented to you, and more inclined to question their validity. In other words you will be more ready to assess whether 'facts' are indeed facts, or simply propaganda. As a result you will have a better and more accurate view of the world around you.

Why do I need to know about it in the first and second years when I only get to do it in the final year?

Again, there is a simple answer, and also a more complex answer.

The simple answer is that you need to prepare for what is going to take up a significant amount of your study time in the final year, working independently, facing difficulties and addressing them yourself. It is much easier if you have been grounded, or grounded yourself by using this book, in what you are expected to do. Starting from scratch when you return to university for the final year is only going to add to your workload in a year when you least need that. By preparing yourself for actually doing the project you can hit the ground running, with a lot of the more reflective tasks, like choosing the topic area for your project, largely behind you. Without this preparation you might waste much of the period before the Christmas break agonising over issues which you could easily have addressed earlier. Wasting time is not something you can afford in the final year!

You might perhaps have wondered why the project is left until the final year. The reasoning is straightforward, and is a result of the different levels of work associated with the three study years of a degree. As you've probably noticed, university is rather different from school. At school, it often seemed that each year was rather like the previous one – you didn't have much sense of progression in what was being asked of you, although you may well have noticed some kind of change when you moved on from GCSEs to A Levels.

Have a look at Table 1.1, which outlines the progression in intellectual demands placed on you in the different years of your degree programme. In the final column you will find an analogy relating to the different jobs you find in medicine. Each of these medical jobs plays a vital role in medicine, but they are progressively more demanding as you go down the table.

TABLE 1.1   The intellectual demands of a degree programme year by year

Year	Basic requirement	More detailed requirement	Medical analogy
1	Describe	Identify key features of case Identify appropriate theory	Junior nurse
2	Describe + **Analyse**	Level 1 + Apply the theory and produce thorough analysis	Senior lab technician
Final	Describe + Analyse + **Synthesise**	Level 2 + Interpret the analysis and make appropriate recommendations, again using appropriate theoretical frameworks	GP (= 2:2) Surgeon (= 2:1) Specialist (= 1st)

Analyse

In the context of your research project, to analyse is to break down a problem systematically in order to understand it better.

The medical analogy helps in making clear what the differences in intellectual demands are.

In Year 1, you are like a junior nurse. You learn basic procedures and how to apply them. You learn the outline of why the procedures have been designed that way, but you have little opportunity for making decisions. Work is fairly standardised, and you have little opportunity to explore particular areas that may interest you.

As a 'senior lab technician' in Year 2, you have more responsibility, more skills and the emphasis in your work is on analysing, in this case samples sent to the lab. You have some responsibility, but not full responsibility. You still work in a way that is based on standard procedures, but you need to give some thought to alternative procedures. Your main task is one of analysis, and you write up the results of that analysis. You don't interpret those results however. You can tell me the precise levels of the cholesterol in my blood, for example, but I wouldn't look to you for a diagnosis – I'd want a *doctor* to interpret the results you've produced.

In your second year you are doing mainly the equivalent work of the senior lab technician, but you are also still doing the work of a junior nurse.

In your final year you are more like the qualified doctor or surgeon. You have a lot more responsibility and you have to make decisions constantly. Often these will be based on the results of analysis conducted by the senior lab technician. With your level of education and training you are able to interpret the results and draw conclusions about what is best for the patient, something which a senior lab technician could not do.

In your final year you are doing mainly the equivalent work of a doctor, but you are still doing the work of both the senior lab technician – you still have to conduct analysis so that you can then conduct synthesis – and the junior nurse – you still have carry out basic procedures in order to set up your analysis.

Synthesise

In the context of your research project, to synthesise is to build up answers systematically to research questions once analysis has been conducted.

Another way to get a sense of this kind of intellectual progression is to consider the three questions a business consultant would seek to answer when investigating a problem in a company:

1. Where did the organisation go wrong?
2. What should they have done?
3. How can they put things right?

> It's pretty clear that as you progress through the three study years of your degree programme, the intellectual demands on you increase significantly. Often this is reflected in how your degree classification is calculated – a typical method is to weight the three years thus: first year marks count 0 per cent; second year marks count 30 per cent; final year marks count 70 per cent.

Your project is thus weighted significantly towards your degree classification because it is an intellectually demanding task, requiring description, analysis and synthesis. In many respects *your* project epitomises all that your degree programme has been leading towards, and, with respect to your degree, it has more of your input than the regular modules in the programme.

Suppose that, as the consultant on a vast fee, all you did was answer the first question. The organisation wouldn't find that terribly helpful – it may well be that they know the answer to this particular question already. And, in any case, your answer may just be a statement of the bleeding obvious.

Answering the second question will be a bit more helpful to them, and they maybe haven't worked that out for themselves. It's the third question that they can't answer, and which they are paying you serious money to answer, respecting your awesome consultancy skills, which they lack.

What is research all about?

Imagine this (entirely imaginary!) conversation between my wife and me.

Me: Someone at work said there are some pretty good flights on offer to Barcelona at the moment. Do you fancy a long weekend there?
She: Sound's great. I'll research it on the internet.

Why do you think my blood would boil?

(A clue – my job title is Honorary Research Fellow)

We've reached an important point in your use of this book. Remember what the light bulb means? To save you looking it up, I'll say it again: 'Stop and be prepared to do some work away from the book. This will involve some personal reflection, and you will need to spend some time thinking'. It's only natural to think, 'Oh, sod that for a game of soldiers, I'll just read on. He's bound to tell me the answer.' You're right that I will tell you the answer, but you've failed to grasp the key point about these 'Stop' mini-exercises. They are designed to get you thinking and learning from the process. If you don't put the time in on thinking, you won't learn by simply jumping to reading the answer. It's a little like using a book to help you learn to drive. If the book says, 'Now go and drive for half an hour remembering what you've just read', it would be pretty stupid to ignore that, and just get on with reading the book.

OK, rant over – I'm going to assume that you have spent some time wondering why I got so grumpy in that particular situation. It was because, when she said, 'I'll do some research on the internet', I felt she was misusing the word research.

Write in your personal definition of the word 'research':

I see the key characteristics of research as:

1. Finding out (discovering) something
2. that is unknown
3. to anyone
4. through a logical process
5. of investigation
6. with a reasonable degree of certainty as to the outcome
7. and publishing the results.

If we assume that my wife would publish the results of her research into cheap air fares to Barcelona (to me at least!), which one of the seven characteristics listed above would not fit with her use of the word research?

Time for self-control! Don't read on until you have had a serious stab at the question!

It's the third one – that research is about finding out something that nobody knows. Obviously somebody knows the information – the airline which has put the details on its

Gap (in the body of knowledge)

Something which nobody knows (yet!).

Contribution

In this context, 'contribution' refers to a contribution to the body of knowledge, in other words, a new piece of knowledge (normally quite a small one) which is the outcome of research.

Literature review

A systematic and critical account of academic research which has already been published. See Chapter 6.

Central research question (CRQ)

The one overall question that encapsulates what you are trying to find out by doing your research.

Methodology

The systematic overall design of your research.

website. Some excellent journalism, for example, is concerned with 'exposing' illegal, unethical or downright immoral practices. Important though investigative journalism is, it isn't strictly research because somebody already knows what's going on – the person(s) the journalist is trying to expose.

The fundamental research process begins by identifying a **gap** in the body of knowledge and proceeding systematically to fill that gap with a **contribution** to the body of knowledge.

Actually, it does sound a bit scary, doesn't it? I need to point out two things:

- The body of knowledge is more riddled with holes than a Swiss cheese.
- For an undergraduate research project, it's only a tiny hole that you are being asked to identify and then fill.

It's worth considering what a famous thinker, Sir Eric Ashby (1961), once said about research in British universities. He described it as 'crawl[ing] along the frontiers of knowledge with a hand-lens'. A 'hand-lens' is just an old-fashioned word for 'magnifying glass', by the way.

Let's go back a sec to the seven characteristics of research given above, and look at the fourth one, 'through a logical process', a bit more.

At the heart of your project will be the following process:

TABLE 1.2 The logical process of conducting your project

1. Identifying a gap in knowledge	This you will achieve by something called a **literature review**.
2. Asking an appropriate **central research question**	If this a poor or inappropriate question, you will be destined to produce a bad answer. If it's a good question, you will be able to answer it by designing an appropriate research **methodology**.
3. Gathering data	This you will achieve either by fieldwork or deskwork.
4. Systematically and logically answering the central research question	This you will achieve by analysis and synthesis of the data.

In the real world, that is, outside universities, people often use the word 'research' to cover the two data- or information-gathering stages of the process – **fieldwork**, which means gathering primary data in the real world through questionnaires, interviews, etc., and **deskwork**, that is, gathering secondary data from cyberspace and/or bashing away at the computer either number-crunching or writing up your work. This is misleading, as research is a larger process than merely fieldwork or deskwork. Fieldwork and deskwork are vital to the research process, but are only a part of it.

One clear point to get hold of right at this early stage is that research is about asking and answering a question. That's definitely something that you are entirely familiar with, but what's different this time is that you have to come up with the question yourself. Your actual question is therefore is vital. A bad question will inevitably lead you to a bad answer, and hence a failed project. A good question, on the other hand, means that a good answer is possible (but not guaranteed).

There is a second clear point to get hold of, especially at this early stage. Doing a project has a lot of uncertainty attached to it. Things may go wrong, but if you've planned your project well, the risks are minimised, and you will already have a Plan B in place to fall back on.

What happens if it all starts to go pear shaped?

Before we get on to what to do if things go pear shaped, we need to think about how things might go wrong and why they might go wrong.

Let's start by considering how doing research is a bit like a sleepwalker trying to find their way home. Bear with me on this!

It would be great if the research process was like leaving your front door and walking in a straight line to the first corner in the road. In one sense it is – it has a clear start and a clear finish. But it's the 'straight line' bit that's the problem.

The research process is indeed a directed process, towards a clear goal, but you will sometimes find yourself accidentally going off at a tangent, and sometimes down a dead end. We will see shortly that there are a number of steps to the research process, and occasionally you may have to go back a step and rethink your next step, a bit like the sleepwalker. They know where home is, but are a bit confused about getting there. Sometimes they go down a cul de sac; sometimes they inadvertently walk round the block and get back to where they were twenty minutes before, but at least they now know which is the wrong way ahead.

Unlike the sleepwalker, you can prepare for problems by having contingency, or fall-back, plans. What you need to be good at is identifying potential problems. Many of these may well be spotted by your project supervisor – when that happens, take heed rather than bury your head in the sand.

I remember a student who wanted to research the very specific travel sector of immigrants and their descendants wanting to return on holiday to a particular country in Africa. This sounded to me to be an interesting and worthwhile topic. Certainly there was a distinct *gap in knowledge*, but I was worried about how she was proposing to gather her data. She said she had two friends who were travel agents specialising in this very small market, and she was sure they would give her the names and addresses of their customers so she could then send them questionnaires and/or interview them.

Deskwork

Conducting the gathering of secondary data. This can be conducted either at a desk in the office, using internet resources, or in a library, using good old books and journals. In contrast, we also speak of 'fieldwork' (see below) for data that we have to go out and gather in a live working environment.

Fieldwork

The gathering of primary data. This cannot be achieved by sitting in your office space or in a library, so to gather primary data you have to go out 'into the field', meaning into the organisation(s) you are researching.

Now this seemed pretty unlikely to happen to me, not least because it would almost certainly involve her friends breaching the Data Protection Act. Would they risk breaking the law and jeopardising their business for the sake of her project? I thought not; she was convinced they would. About a fortnight before she was due to hand in her project she came to see me, and was very upset to admit that she had finally given up twisting her friends' arms to break the law, and in fact it was now too late to make contact with sufficient numbers of eligible people to interview. If she'd had a Plan B ready, she might just have recovered it.

If I had a pound for every time one of my Sports Management students had announced they were going to interview the twenty chairmen of the Premier League clubs, I could easily afford a Championship ticket. It's never going to happen because they will not speak to respected journalists, let alone students. Similarly, if I'd had a pound for every time a Tourism Management student had said that they planned to use questionnaires at a local airport, failing to realise that they would be detained by security the minute they did, I would be afloat in pies and Bovril at all those Championship games.

What I'm driving at is the possibility that the vast majority of problems can be foreseen with a little bit of thought, and a little bit of discussion with your supervisor. The minute such a risk is recognised, you should develop at least the outline of a Plan B. Above all, you need to think to think about when the problem might arise, and what the implications of this would be for your Plan B.

Iterative

An iterative process is one which reaches its intended goal through repetition, typically by finding better and better approximations. See Figure 1.1.

Research should also be thought of as an **iterative** process. I see you reaching for the dictionary, so let me explain. An iterative process is one which consists of seeking better and better approximations to a perfect solution. Figure 1.1 below gives a clear and simple example of an iterative process.

Guess the number – an iterative process

Suppose you ask someone to think of a number between 1 and 50, and then you try to find out what that number is by asking Yes/No questions.

A scatter-gun approach would be to ask questions like 'Is it 43? Is it 6? Is it 32?' And so on. You might strike lucky early on, but on average it will take you 25 goes to get the right answer.

An iterative approach would be as follows. Let's assume the number is 17. The questioning would go like this:

    Is the number more than 25? No.
    Is the number between 1 and 12 inclusive? No.
    Is the number between 13and 19 inclusive? Yes.
    Is the number between 13 and 16 inclusive? No.
    Is the number either 17 or 18? Yes.
    Is the number 17? Yes.

FIGURE 1.1   Example of an iterative process

Using this iterative approach, each time refining your view by getting a better approximation, you can find out the number in six questions, which is definitely a better approach than the scatter-gun one. In a few cases the scatter-gun approach will work better, but those will be when Lady Luck is definitely on your side. The iterative approach is a design which in general reduces the risk of you having to go on and on asking questions. To put it another way, by adopting an iterative approach you have designed a strategy that reduces the risk of having to carry on asking questions for too long.

Overall the message is: reduce risk by good research design, anticipate the 'unexpected' and make sure you already have a fall-back strategy prepared in outline. Research very rarely falls out neatly according to your first plan. Accept the fact that changes in your original plan are likely to be forced upon you. Don't be thrown into a state of panic by this – be prepared!

How will I be able to tell if my project is any good?

That may seem at first sight to be a strange question at this point, when you haven't even started to write your project. But remember, we have just learned that good design will lead to a more effective research process, and hence to a better project.

If you know at the start how it is going to be judged at the end, you can build in a kind of quality control as you go along. The checklist below shows the kind of quality control system that will be applied by the lecturers marking your project once you have completed it. Not all of it will immediately make sense to you, so keep coming back to it as a check-list as you get deeper and deeper into working on your project.

 Some questions that markers will be asking

Introduction

Is the context well explained?

Is it clear why the research is worthwhile?

Literature review

Have you clearly identified a gap in knowledge?

Have you read widely enough?

(Continued)

Aims

In the context of your research project, an aim is a middle-level member of the research design hierarchy. Aims are derived from the central research question, and lead on to research objectives. See page 75.

Objectives

In this context, 'research objective' as opposed to 'personal objective'. The lowest and most specific layer of the research design hierarchy, research objectives are derived from aims. See page 75.

(Continued)

Have you identified the theory areas that are relevant? Are they the most relevant?

Have you noted any limits on applying particular frameworks?

Central research question

Is there a central research question that has driven your work? Has it been clearly stated?

Is it answerable by research?

Aims and objectives

Have the **aims** and **objectives** been clearly stated?

Have they been used to help develop your project?

Have they been referred to as you have written up your project?

Methodology

Have you used an appropriate approach to answer your central research question?

Have you justified your choice of approach? Have you justified not using other approaches?

Have you correctly recognised how specific or how general the outcomes of your research will be?

Have you correctly recognised what the relevant issues and concepts are?

Analysis

Have you been rigorous in your analysis? Does your argument flow logically from data to conclusions?

Is your reasoning clear, straightforward and correct?

Have you made appropriate comparisons?

Conclusions

Are your conclusions appropriate? More specifically, do they relate to your stated aims and objective*s*? Do they answer your central research question?

Have you made appropriate recommendations?

Have you realised the implications of your research?

Have you acknowledged any limitations?

Project presentation

Have you acknowledged the sources of the frameworks?

Have you referenced all sources in the text?

Have you used a consistent and adequate referencing system?

Is your report well structured and in a natural order?

Is the abstract accurate?

Are the spelling and grammar acceptable?

Overall

Is there a strong logical flow?

Do the chapters hang together well as a whole?

Are the chapters well linked?

Are your conclusions convincing?

Is there a jointly authored journal article here which could be produced?

If you use the questions above honestly in the last weeks before you hand your project in, you should not only be able to tell with a reasonable degree of accuracy whether you are going to pass or fail, but you should also get some idea of the grade you are going to get.

You are probably going to have access in your intranet site for the project module to a guide on the grades that are awarded. I've given an example of this below as Table 1.3.

What is the message that underlies these guidelines? You can find themes which are repeated at the different levels. In this case they are:

- structure and design of the project
- the internal logic of following a hierarchy of central research question, aims and objectives
- the power of the analysis and synthesis
- whether or not there is 'added value'
- the quality of your communication skills.

You may find these in your university's guidelines on the grading of projects, and you may find other themes, for example, evidence of how widely you have read in academic journals.

TABLE 1.3 Example of grade criteria

First 70–100	The project is well structured and communicated. It has an overall and consistent logic that makes the conclusions compelling. Excellent with respect to 'value added' through competent research.
	For a mark of 80+ the project should be of sufficient standard to have the potential to make a contribution to the wider academic world.
Two-one (upper second) 60–69	Each element for the project has been well designed and executed. Overall, however, the result is somewhat disjointed. Clear evidence of independent inquiry and critical judgement in selecting, ordering, analysing and synthesising. Confidence may be placed in the conclusions. High on 'value added'.
Two-two (lower second) 50–59	Aims and objectives set out. Some appropriate theory plus an attempt at analysis and with basic linkage between theory and analysis. Conclusions are consistent with the evidence presented but are not compelling. Some 'value added'.
Third 40–49	Makes only a basic attempt to answer a central research question. Lacks focus and only a weak attempt at analysis. Limited 'value added'.
Marginal fail 35–39	Fails to ask and/or answer a central research question. Essentially descriptive work showing only limited understanding and application of ideas. No 'value added'. Tending towards being an extended essay. No evidence that relevant subject knowledge has been understood.
Poor fail 0–34	Poorly organised superficial description with virtually no understanding or analysis of the issues involved. No attempt at synthesis. No evidence of having understood the research process. An extended essay rather than an evidence-based research output.

Print off your university's equivalent of Table 1.3 above. Go through it carefully and identify the themes, or, to put it another way, what Captain Subtext is saying. Write your list of themes here:

That's covered the assessment of how good your project is that you can do yourself. But there is one other source of assessment that you should take seriously: your project supervisor. The quality of his/her assessment of how well your project is shaping up depends on how well they know what you are doing and planning. It's clear that you should:

- meet your project supervisor regularly
- be open and honest about the state of your project
- listen to their advice
- take that advice on board.

Your supervisor needs to know what progress you have and haven't made, so it is a good idea to send them by email whatever you have written a few days before each meeting. They will give better feedback if they have had a chance to read through your work before you meet rather than comment on a wad of paper you have just shoved across their desk.

How relevant is this project to working in the real world?

Before looking at the real world, there are a number of possibilities in the university world you might want to think about.

It's not unknown for a really good undergraduate business project to be worked up with your supervisor into a co-authored journal article for publication. I've done it myself, although on very few occasions, so be realistic – it *could* happen, but the chances are stacked against this happening.

If you are even vaguely thinking of going on to do a Masters degree, you will need to have a good first degree under your belt, which makes writing a good project especially important. On a Masters degree programme you will have to produce a dissertation, which is similar to the project you are doing now on an undergraduate programme, but on an extended scale. It will be of a greater length than the project, and you will be expected to analyse and synthesise more deeply. So, all the research skills and competences which you will develop for your project will set you up well for writing your Masters dissertation. In fact, most Masters courses include a module on much the same subjects that we are covering here!

Let's now turn briefly away from the world of academia and what Tom Lehrer (1990), an American satirist, once described in a song as 'ivy-covered professors in ivy-covered halls' to the real world of gainful employment and jobs.

If you leave university after your Bachelors degree, you will probably never again write anything as long and complex as your project. In twenty years working in the private sector, I was never called upon to write a research report that could be compared to a project. If such a report was needed, for example, market research into a possible new product, it was outsourced to a market research company. On the other hand, I often had to research particular subjects, such as the state of competition in the business sector which I was working in, and write similar reports to a project. Normally they were in a different format to the rigid structure required for a project, but I was only able to write them because of the research skills and competences I had developed, which were almost the same as those you are developing here. In a nutshell, you will find the skills and competences developed now very useful in the real world – they will give you a chance to impress your boss – but you are unlikely to write a report which has the feel of an undergraduate research project.

One particular difference you will find is with what is called the abstract in your project, which in the real world becomes an executive summary. With your project, it is the whole project that is read and considered, but in the real world, most people who read the executive summary will then only dip into the relevant bits of the report you have produced. The skill of writing effective executive summaries is thus slightly different from that of writing an abstract for your project, and you will have to adapt accordingly. Now is not the time to worry about that though!

 To finish off the work in this section, it's time for you to try the first of the exercises designed to develop your research skills and competences (on the next page).

Chapter conclusion

Let's just pause and take stock of where we have reached.

We have worked on:

- the importance of the project to you
- what you will get out of doing a good project
- how the project fits into the three-year Bachelor programme
- what research is
- coping with the difficulties that will come up while doing your project
- making sure, as you go along, that you are writing a project that will be successful
- a quick look at how the project will be of relevance after you graduate and go into the real world of business.

Before we move on to the next section, which is about actually beginning your research, it's time to jot down your first thoughts about the topic you are choosing to research. This is not an undertaking that can be taken lightly.

My first thoughts on my choice of topic:

- Industry sector and geographical area, or specific company

  e.g. Japanese car manufacture in Britain, bed and breakfast businesses in Tiverton, Virgin Trains, Manchester United Football Club

- Business function

  e.g. marketing, finance, human resource management, strategy

These really should be just your first thoughts. Once you have them, you are in a good position to have your first meeting with your supervisor. Your supervisor may spot some obvious pitfalls which will help shape your second thoughts. For example, if a student came to me with any of the first thoughts in the box above, I would advise against a project on Manchester United. Why? Well, it has already been widely researched and so it would be difficult to find a gap in knowledge. Also there are likely to be problems of access – they are flooded with requests for access from business research projects and not particularly cooperative because of these numbers. Virgin, on the other hand, are much more student friendly, and provide a 'student project pack' on their website. The downside of this is that many students have been there before you, and it will be difficult to find a gap in knowledge.

Have you completed all the exercises and write-in boxes in Section 1? If you haven't, you should do so before you move on to Section 2, where you will be 'Beginning your Research'.

SECTION 2

Beginning Your Research

Section guide

So far you will have covered a general introduction to the world of research but we have not yet looked in any depth at how this is applied to your project. In this part, you will look more deeply at the project, how it will be structured, the support you can expect and the question of **ethics** in your approach to your project. At the end of this section, you will learn about the two basic approaches to research, and you will be asked to reflect on which you feel more comfortable with. In later sections we will consider how the choice of which approach you feel more comfortable with has implications for the design of your research project, and what you can and cannot do as a result.

Ethics

The principles of what is right and what is wrong.

In Section 2 you will work your way through to the answers to the following questions:

1. What's the basic idea then?
   How and why the project is structured the way it is.
2. So that's the same for everyone, is it?
   The basic similarities and differences between all students' projects – the difference between 'process' and 'content'.
3. Are there any other differences?
   The two basic approaches to research.
4. But what exactly will I have to hand in?
   The technical specification and an outline of the required structure.
5. What support will I get?
   The formal support through lectures and seminars, and from your supervisor.
6. How should I go about choosing my topic?
   A simple framework for brainstorming possibilities and then choosing a clear topic.
7. Right, I've got at least the first version of my central research question – isn't it a bit airy-fairy?
   Refining or tweaking your central research question into a form that has the best potential to produce a good project.

8. Can I just go ahead and ask anyone anything I need to?
   The limitations that ethical issues impose on what is or isn't possible and/or practical.
9. This all sounds a bit, well, philosophical, but it's real world business we're talking about, isn't it?
   How doing your project doesn't really relate to the real world of business.
10. So when would this sort of approach be appropriate in business?
    How doing your project does relate to, and prepare you for, the real world of business.
11. Does this mean there are two different 'processes', one for each of the two approaches?
    How the two approaches share some characteristics and yet also have distinct differences.

2

The Basic Idea

Chapter objectives

By completing the work in this chapter, you should be able to:

- explain what a research project really is
- understand the principle of identifying a central research question
- identify the differences between research 'process' and project 'content'
- appreciate the two basic research perspectives
- assess which research perspective is the more natural one for you to follow.

Introduction

In this chapter we begin by exploring how and why the project is structured the way it is. In doing this, the logic underlying the structure will begin to emerge, and you should start to appreciate not only how the various parts of your Project will fit together, but also why the correct design is needed to get this to happen.

Next we will explore what makes your Project unique, its content, and what is essentially the same for everyone doing the Project, the process.

Finally, we start to look at some basic alternatives to do with conducting research, ones which derive from the way you see the world. To give you a taster of this, think about whether you tend to see issues in terms of black and white, or in terms of shades of grey.

What's the basic idea then?

Now we will look at the basic structure of what you will be doing. There will be more detail on each stage in future chapters, but resist any temptation to jump ahead – it's important that you have a basic understanding of the overall process before you start diving into detail.

Identify a gap in existing knowledge

What is known by society in general, rather than what you as an individual happen to know, forms something known as 'the body of knowledge'. However knowledgeable you happen to be, your personal knowledge will always be less than the body of knowledge – nobody ever knows everything. I certainly don't know everything!

What you are hoping to achieve with your research project is a contribution to the body of knowledge. It won't be a contribution if somebody else already knows, so one of the first things you need to consider is whether what you are trying to find out will actually make a contribution – it won't if somebody else already knows but you didn't happen to be aware of it. For example, it wouldn't make sense if you planned as your contribution to find out how much profit Virgin Atlantic made in the last five years – probably you don't know this as you sit there reading this book, but certainly somebody does, and with a little bit of searching on the internet or in the library you could find out what the figure is.

So, if you are going to make a real contribution, you have to make sure before you start that what you are trying to find out is unknown to everybody. Bear in mind the kind of thing you are trying to find out – it's going to be something within that general body of knowledge which is in the part of the body labelled 'business and management'. It follows that you will need to look pretty closely to see exactly what is already known and what is not known in the area of 'business and management'.

A pretty daunting task, you might cry! But your chosen topic will cut down the scope of what you need to look at within 'business and management'. You'll probably have chosen one of the subject areas you are enjoying on your degree programme so far – let's say, for example, it's 'marketing'. As you develop your choice of topic, it will progress to a specific part of 'marketing' – let's say 'public relations' for the sake of argument. Now the part of the body of knowledge which is 'public relations' is smaller than the part which is 'marketing', which is in turn smaller than the part which is 'business and management'. So, by refining your choice of topic you are focusing in on a relatively small part of the body of knowledge, and by doing this you are closing down the area of your search to discover what is known and what is not known.

Now is the time to start thinking more deeply about this. Your choice will have two dimensions – a) the part of 'business and management' that appeals to you and which you are good at, and b) a sector of industry. For example, you might choose a) human resource management and b) the airline industry.

Where do you look? The most obvious place is where research findings are published – academic journals. In the old days, even searching in, for example, marketing journals which covered public relations would have been a problem. Either you would have had to plough systematically through shelf after shelf of journals in your university library, or you would have come to the conclusion that the library didn't have copies of the particular journal(s) you should have been looking in. Fortunately for you, not only is there the internet, but your university library will have subscriptions to online databases of academic journals – for example, Ebsco. If you don't know what is available through your e-library, find out now as a matter of urgency – fellow students may well be able to give you a quick steer, but it is always best to check with the specialist subject librarian. He or she will be able to point you to specialist online databases as well as the more common ones.

You thus need to do what is called a literature search (but this is in fact the first part of a literature review, a rather important distinction which we will return to in Chapter 6). Using key word searches, you will be able to establish just what exactly is known, which determines what is *not* known – and therefore what possibilities there are for you to find out something new. To use the jargon, you are identifying a gap in knowledge. When you have completed your research and written it up as your Project, you will have filled that gap, and made a contribution to the body of knowledge.

Remember that you are not required to make an enormous contribution – you are not expected to be the Einstein of business and management.

Nonetheless, what we are looking for is a small contribution. The fact that you will have made a contribution by the end of the academic year is something you will be able to be proud about.

Choose a research question

When we talk of making a contribution, we beg the question of how you go about this. The answer to that question can be reduced to a single idea – asking and answering a *central research question* – more on this in Chapter 4, when we will look at what are and aren't valid central research questions, and what makes good or bad central research questions.

What is important at this stage, when you haven't actually formulated your CRQ, is that you appreciate just how important the CRQ is in the whole process.

The gap in knowledge will shape the kind of CRQ you ask, and the quality of your answer will shape your contribution.

Each of the three words in 'central research question' is significant:

- **Central**

  There will be a whole range of questions that will emerge as you design the process of your research project. What you need to do is make sure that they all fall within one over-arching question. This, the CRQ, defines the scope of what you will be doing. At any time over the next months when you are working on your project, you should stop and ask yourself, 'Is what I'm doing now helping me to answer my CRQ?' If the answer is 'Yes!', then you are working on the right lines. If the answer is 'No!', however, there are two possibilities – either stop what you are doing because you have drifted away from what you have set yourself as your task and you are wasting your valuable time, or tweak your CRQ slightly so that the answer becomes 'Yes!'. That last course of action may, at first glance, seem a bit of a bodge. It isn't – it's part of what we saw above is the iterative nature of research (see page 14).

- **Research**

  The question you ask must be answerable by research. For example, 'Does God exist?' or 'What is the meaning of life?' are fascinating questions, but they aren't answerable through the kind of research process you will be using. (And of course they are also nothing to do with business and management!)

- **Question**

  I start to get seriously worried when I ask one of my own students, 'What's your CRQ?' and get a reply like, 'Oh, something to do with the petroleum industry and finance'. Call me Percy Pickie but 'something to do with' isn't a question!!! Remember, if you are not asking a question, you are not going to get an answer. It is the asking and answering of a question that is at the heart of what you are supposed to be doing. One particular advantage of using this method of asking and answering a question is that you know when your research is complete – when you've fully answered the central research question!

Produce a research design

It's only once you have got at least a first draft of your central research question that you can start to decide how you are going to answer that question. I mean, you wouldn't start to sketch out in notes how you were going to compose an essay or a report if you hadn't been told what the question was, would you? If you answered 'Yes!', I despair!

To create your research design you will need to work on the following:

- aims and objectives
- establishing a methodology
- choosing appropriate **methods**.

Methods

The research tools that are used to gather your data, such as questionnaires or interviews.

Let's look at these in outline at this stage, and return to them in more detail in later chapters as your Project moves forward.

The aims and objectives flow from the central research question via the methodology to the research you will undertake in terms of gathering information and then processing it to produce conclusions. They are the key to developing a sense of logical flow in what you do, and in building the case that your conclusion(s) are unarguable. They form a hierarchy of logic and its application.

The central research question is essentially conceptual. It does not necessarily give an indication of how it will be answered. It does, however, identify the gap in knowledge you will fill and hence make a contribution.

Your Project will have one central research question.

Aims are a mix of conceptual and practical. They begin to move the central research question towards the specific research you plan to undertake. They break the central research question into perhaps two, or at most three, lines of investigation, with probably a hint of how you will proceed.

Objectives break each aim into specific research objectives, translatable into real world research or, in other words, objectives which can be put into practice in a relatively obvious way.

For the moment you don't need to have a perfect understanding of how aims and objectives differ. We will return to this in more detail, and on page 75 I will lead you through a couple of examples of how this hierarchy evolves, showing how the elements are linked together, and how, overall, you can build an awesome logic into your research design.

So that's the same for everyone, is it?

In one sense, yes, but, in another sense, no!

To make sense out of the last sentence, we need to distinguish between the two ideas of 'process' and 'content'. Research is a process, which has a content.

The process relates to how a project (any project) is done. It is what constitutes the common factor between all your projects.

The content is what distinguishes your project from all others.

This book is designed for all students to use, and is therefore centred on the process of doing a research project. What makes it different from other books is that it is designed to help you relate *your* content to that general process. As you work your way through the book, the write-in sections are designed for you to customise the general process to match your intended content.

The balance between process and content will change as you progress through your project. At first you will need to focus much more on process. This is because it is in the early stages that you produce your design for doing research.

The danger is that you may begin by wanting to focus on content. In a way, this is a natural reaction – after all, it's your project you want to focus on rather than on some generalised 'one-size-fits-all' type of project. It's a very dangerous reaction though – if you don't start by focusing on process, you won't develop a sound research design; without that, your project will go badly wrong.

As your project develops and you put your research design into action, the content becomes your major focus. The two, process and content, are interlinked through your design, and so the two are never quite separate. Figure 2.1 shows how the balance typically shifts over time.

Take note that the line dividing process from content does not begin or finish in the corners – even at the start of doing your project you need to give some thought to content, and even at the finish you need to give some thought to process. Also note that the line is a dashed one, to show that the two are interconnected to some extent.

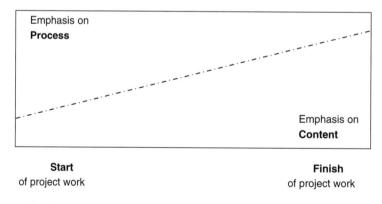

FIGURE 2.1   The changing balance between process and content

Remember, in a nutshell:

1. Process

That which is the same for all projects:

The process of doing research.

2. Content

That which distinguishes your project from other projects:

The content of *your* project.

Are there any other differences?

It would be too easy if there weren't, wouldn't it?

There are two different approaches to the design of research, reflecting different perspectives or **paradigm**s of the world and how we operate in it. So far I've largely managed to avoid using some of the heavier terminology of research, but in looking at these two perspectives it becomes inevitable that I have to introduce some heavy terminology. This is one of those lucky cases where the two concepts are pretty easy to understand and are clearly different. I'm therefore going to get the concepts over to you before I give them their slightly scary 'labels' or names.

To help you understand, we'll begin with a little self-assessment exercise.

 Stop and circle the word from each pair of words you feel more comfortable with. You may need to spend some time thinking, but, for most people, the choice is obvious.

Words *or* Numbers

Arts *or* Sciences

Next, when making judgements, do you tend to see things as being in:

Shades of grey *or* Black and white?

Finally, do you think of the world outside as:

A different world for each of us *or* One single world for all of us?

Paradigm

A consistent set of thoughts and practices which together may be seen as a way of viewing the world. Scientists, for example, talk of Einstein overthrowing the older Newtonian paradigm when he produced his Theory of Relativity. There are two major research paradigms – positivist and phenomenological.

Most of us will tend to have marked words either on the left of the column or on the right. As we shall see, which side we have tended towards shows us to be more comfortable with

Hermeneutic, Interpretivist, Phenomenological

Although these words do have slightly different meanings, for our purposes we can consider them as having the same meaning: words used as a label for the word-based, qualitative, arts-oriented research paradigm.

Positivist

'Positivist' is, for our purposes, a word used as a label for the number-based, quantitative, science-oriented research paradigm.

one or other of the two research perspectives. Let's take what might appear to be a giant leap but is in fact a small step and give those two perspectives names, and set out in a bit more detail what they stand for (see Table 2.1).

TABLE 2.1   The two research processes

Phenomenological perspective[1] (also known as Hermeneutic or Interpretivist perspective)	Positivist perspective
We each see different worlds outside our heads.	One single world exists outside our heads.
There are no universal rules that can be applied in every situation.	We can measure the reality of that world scientifically, independently and objectively.
There are different views of business and management held by different groups such as marketers and accountants.	That world can be explained by universal laws and truths.
We agree through general consensus.	We agree because we all see the same truth.
The study and practice of business and management is largely an art.	The study and practice of business and management is largely a science.

[1]It's perhaps not surprising that a perspective which sees a single world has a single name – positivist – while a perspective that sees multiple worlds can have one of several names. They have slightly different meanings, but this should not bother us in the context of an undergraduate research project. I will stick with one of them – 'phenomenological'.

Remember, the words may be unfamiliar and rather off-putting, but they are just words – convenient labels for ideas. In a similar way, you might think about how the word 'logic' is a convenient label for a process that is quite difficult to describe but has a clear enough meaning for us to use the word without being worried about how we would explain it each time we use it.

Again, stop and reflect:

 Which of these two perspectives do you feel more comfortable with? Totally one or the other?

If you are a positivist, you will probably have written in simply 'positivist', but if you are a phenomenologist you may well have written something like 'mainly phenomenological, although sometimes I am a bit positivist. It depends a lot on circumstances'. From my experience, very few people feel 100 per cent comfortable with either of the two labels, but, on the other hand, very few people find themselves equally torn between the two – we all tend to be more one than the other.

'Why does this actually matter?' you cry!

It matters, and matters seriously, because your research perspective shapes your research methodology, and hence your choice of research methods.

Supposing your research design is aimed at evaluating the opinions of a particular group of people – middle managers in the financial services industry or supermarket customers, for example.

There are two ways you might go about this. One method is by interviewing people from that group, and the other is by getting people from that group to fill in questionnaires where they have to mark on a scale from 1 (strongly disagree) to 5 (strongly agree), something which is known as a Likert scale.

The first method produces lots of words as the outcome (in other words, it's a **qualitative method**) whereas the second method produces lots of numbers (in other words, it's a **quantitative method**). The first method is appropriate if your research perspective is phenomenological, whereas the second method is appropriate if your research method is positivist. To put it in a general way, your perspective leads you to an appropriate methodology, and this has its own set of appropriate methods. We are beginning to see what is one of the keys to creating a good research design – an awesome consistency and logic which pervades the design (see Figure 2.2).

It's worth noting, nonetheless, in case you haven't spotted it, that questionnaires can be used to produce quantitative evidence (in other words, lots of words) by asking open-ended questions, where respondents fill in their own answers, rather than by asking them to quantify their feelings via a Likert scale.

Don't worry if you are still a little unsure about which research perspective is the appropriate one for you, or about what exactly research methodology and research methods are. We will look again at these topics in more detail in later chapters.

For the moment, let's look a little further at some other overall different approaches you can take in deciding on your research design.

Are there still more differences?

When approaching any kind of research, there is an underlying assumption that we don't know what the outcome will be. However, that is not to say that we don't have any idea

Qualitative

Pertaining to words. Qualitative data is often referred to as 'soft data'. Qualitative research is more appropriate in researching complex situations which are unlikely to produce precise solutions.

Quantitative

Pertaining to numbers. Quantitative data is often referred to as 'hard data'. Quantitative research is more appropriate in researching straightforward situations which are likely to produce precise solutions.

```
RESEARCH PERSPECTIVE
        ↓
RESEARCH METHODOLOGY
        ↓
RESTRICTED CHOICE OF RESEARCH METHODS
```

FIGURE 2.2   A simple model of research design

what it will be. Frequently researchers make a guess, forming a hypothesis – a statement of the possible outcome. This hypothesis then becomes something which your research is designed to prove to be true, a process called verification. An alternative approach is to try and prove that a hypothesis is false.

Suppose that you are trying to prove that some phenomenon, A, is the cause of some other phenomenon, B. This may well be straightforward if the relationship is actually a straightforward one. Often the cause of phenomenon B will be more complicated – it may be caused by both phenomenon A and another phenomenon, C, or it may be that a further phenomenon, D, causes A and it also causes B. If that is the case, there will be a statistical correlation between A and B, but showing that that is the case tells us nothing about causation nor indeed even involves the true cause, D. In that kind of situation it may be more realistic to show that A does *not* cause B, a process called falsification.

In practice, verification is a more helpful approach, simply because it shows something to be true, closing out other possibilities; falsification may be more realistic but less helpful – we haven't got nearer the truth; we have only eliminated a possibility. If you choose to try and prove that a hypothesis is false, it is only helpful if you manage to come up with a result that is surprising. It would be easy enough to show that the changing price of a loaf of bread is unconnected to the number of flights that Ryanair operates, but it would not exactly be a valuable piece of research, simply because any normal person would have suspected that to be the case.

To put it another way, good research has an element of surprise in its outcome. It is that element of surprise that has a bearing on whether you decide to try to verify or falsify a hypothesis. Bear in mind that you can research the same topic by either approach – all you need to do to swap from one approach to the other is insert or remove the word 'not' from your hypothesis. My general advice would be to stick to the more frequent approach, verification, unless you have good reason to opt for a falsification approach.

Our final pair of approaches to research to consider is the choice of either testing a theory or generating a theory. Undergraduate research is far more likely to involve testing a theory. Generating a theory is a much more challenging choice and involves a much higher risk to your success. It should only be considered in those rare circumstances where your literature research suggests that absolutely no one has ever done any relevant research before you. A far safer approach is to test an established theory in an area where it has not been tested before. For example, you may find a marketing theory that an academic has established on the basis of research in one particular industry sector – it would make good sense, as an undergraduate research project, to test it in another sector.

In a nutshell, the vast majority of undergraduate business research is based on verifying rather than falsifying a hypothesis, and on testing an existing theory in a new set of circumstances rather than on generating a new one.

Chapter conclusion

In this chapter we have covered the following key concepts:

- a gap in the body of knowledge
- choosing a central research question
- producing a research design
- process v. content
- the two research perspectives: phenomenological and positivist; and how you are likely to be more naturally drawn to one rather than the other.

Stop and reflect on these topics. Use the above list as a kind of 'checklist of under-standing' to see whether or not you are ready to go on to the next chapter – go back a few pages and follow the text again if you are still unclear about the basics of the concepts involved. You don't need to be 100 per cent confident in your understanding as we will be going over them again in a bit more depth.

Make sure you have reflected on each fill-in box, and that you have actually committed a response to paper.

If you've reflected fully, and I really mean fully, you're ready to move on to the next chapter.

Recommended reading

Allard-Poesi, F. and Maréchal, C. (2001) 'Constructing the Research Problem' in R.-A. Thietart et al., *Doing Management Research*, London: Sage.

3

Managing the Research Project

Chapter objectives

By completing the work in this chapter, you should be able to:

- give the details of your university's technical specification for the research project
- explain the reasoning behind the standard structure of a research project
- understand the role of your supervisor, and in particular what you can expect and what you cannot expect of him/her.

Introduction

So far we have looked at the undergraduate project in fairly broad terms. Now we need to focus rather more sharply on your project. Here is a question that may well be troubling you.

But what exactly will I have to hand in?

This is of course a question that I can't give you a specific answer for – it will vary from university to university, and even from degree programme to degree programme within a university. What I can do is help you make sure that you find out exactly what it is you have to hand in.

Let's start with the *technical format*

You should be able to find this either from a handout you been given or from the relevant part of your course intranet.

Your own course specification may not have all the detail I will mention, so in some cases I will suggest a default specification. It is exactly that, and not an alternative to your official version!

Get a printed copy of the specification for your degree programme, and, with it in front of you, write in what is required in the boxes below. This may seem overkill to you, but it will help in giving a clear picture of what is required, and, by writing it down, it will help you recognise some of the pickier detail, all of which will be considered important by your university.

Let's begin with what might be called the 'technical specification'.

 Stop and write in your personal answers now.

1. Word or page length:
   a) Maximum length:
   b) Minimum length:

2. What is included in and excluded from the word count?
   a) Included:
   b) Excluded:

3. Specified font:
4. Specified margins:
   a) Top and bottom:
   b) Left and right:

5. Spacing:
   a) Line:
   b) Before:
   c) After:
   d) Line spacing:

6. Single- or double-sided printing?
7. Standard cover design?
8. Standard declaration of originality?
9. Standard binding?
10. To be bound:
    a) by (does your university specify who must bind it?):
    b) before (a certain date):

11. Number of copies required? Remember that this is the number of copies for the university. If you want a copy for yourself, or for your mum and dad, you will need to add these to the numbers you get bound.

Next, you need to check out any requirement for submitting your project online

Plagiarism

The passing off of someone else's work as your own, either deliberately and wilfully (a form of cheating), or accidentally, through failure to cite and reference properly.

Increasingly universities require you to submit your project for checking to anti-**plagiarism** websites such as Turnitin (see http://submit.ac.uk/en_gb/support-services). Typically universities will have already set up an account for you, and you should follow the instructions they will provide you with if this e-submission is necessary.

Some universities allow you a trial e-submission, but others just allow you the one final submission.

Stop and write in your personal answers now.

Does my course require e-submission?

To the university?

To Turnitin or another anti-plagiarism website?

If yes to either of the last questions, how do I submit electronically?

Finally, we need to look at how your project should be *structured*

Stop and write in your personal answers now.

Does your degree project have a defined structure? In other words, is there an 'official list of contents or chapter headings'? If so, write them in below.

If your degree programme doesn't provide one, in Table 3.1 is a default outline (remember, it's not an alternative to your official version). It gives a rationale as to what the different sections consist of.

What support will I get?

Of course, this is going to vary from university to university, and from course to course, but is likely to consist of the following:

- a set of lead lectures on research methodology
- a requirement to submit a proposal, and feedback on this
- a personal supervisor.

Needless to say, attending the lead lectures and any related seminars cannot be recommended too strongly. If you've missed any sessions, make sure you get all the handouts and other material from your university intranet.

There are two issues associated with your supervisor – the choice of academic as your supervisor and what you can reasonably expect, and, equally importantly, what you cannot reasonably expect, from your supervisor.

The allocation of supervisors is made within a number of constraints. Your criteria in choosing your supervisor (if you are able to do so – practice varies from university to university) would probably be:

- Do I get on well with that lecturer?
- Does that lecturer have a good knowledge about my proposed subject area?

On the other hand, from the lecturers' perspective, the criteria are likely to be:

- How many projects has each lecturer been allocated on his/her timetable?
- How experienced in research and in supervising research projects are the individual lecturers in the team?
- Does the lecturer get on passably well with you?

TABLE 3.1   Default project outline structure

Rationale	Outcome
Need to explain the context and why the topic is interesting.	Introduction
Need to identify the gap in knowledge and hence the intended contribution.	Literature review
Need to specify the theoretical frameworks which will be used for analysis and synthesis.	
Need to specify the central research question, and the aims and objectives of the research.	Methodology and methods
Need to define and justify the chosen process of answering the question – broadly and specifically.	
Need to report the results, the analysis of those results and the synthesis derived from the analysis.	Main body
Need to draw from the analysis any conclusions regarding answering the central research question.	Conclusions

With these quite different sets of variables, it will not necessarily follow that you will get the supervisor you want. What then can you do to increase your chances of getting the one you want?

Well, nothing in a formal sense, but informally you may be able to influence the decision of which lecturer you get. The way to do this is by engaging your target lecturer with your as yet vague ideas on what you want to research. Approach your target lecturer and run your first thoughts past them. If you can get them excited about your subject area and what contribution you want to make to the body of knowledge, and convince them, without pestering, that you are a serious and sensible student, you will increase the chances that they will ask the project module leader lecturer to allocate you to them.

Given that each lecturer will only have a finite number of students allocated to them on their timetable, the earlier you flag up your interest to your 'chosen one', the greater your chances of success.

Once you have had your supervisor allocated to you, what can you expect of him/her?

For once, the clue is not in the name – their role is not really one of 'supervising' you. You have the psychological ownership of your project and the responsibility of producing it. The most zealous of supervisors might drift towards a supervising role, but it would probably be more accurate if they were designated as 'adviser' rather than 'supervisor'.

In other words, the onus of consulting with the supervisor is on you.

It is especially important to liaise with the supervisor in the early stages of the project. Remember that the supervisor is not a source of inspiration – you must provide that.

Perhaps the most important part of the supervisor's role is to approve your central research question and your methodology. You will need to justify what you plan to do, and why you have chosen to do it a particular way.

It is not part of the supervisor's role to read lengthy and/or rough submissions.

Remember that lecturers are people too – they often take holidays at Easter and during August, i.e. directly before hand-in dates. You shouldn't be needing to see them at this stage in any case!

You should keep a log of meetings with your supervisor – The appendix contains a write-in template for doing this. This log could prove vital if you were called to attend a Viva (see page 134), so it is really important to keep a full and accurate log just in case you need it at this possible later Viva stage. Thinking about your next meeting with your supervisor is really important, and your log of previous meetings, especially the last one, can be very useful. You should have a clear idea of the agenda you want. If you have questions, try to pre-plan some possible answers as a basis for discussion.

In short, you need to manage the relationship with your supervisor. See the supervisor as a resource.

Now we've covered the basics of the research process, it's time to turn to the content of your project. The place to start is with choosing your research topic.

Chapter conclusion

In this chapter we have covered the following key concepts:

- the technical specification for your research project
- the structure of a research project and the rationale for this
- the role of your supervisor.

Again, as in Chapter 2, stop and reflect on these topics. Use the above list as a kind of 'checklist of understanding' to see whether or not you are ready to go on to the next chapter – go back a few pages and follow the text again if you are still unclear about the basics of the concepts involved. You don't need to be 100 per cent confident in your understanding as we will be going over them again in a bit more depth.

Make sure you have reflected on each fill-in box, and that you have actually committed a response to paper.

4

Choosing the Research Topic

Chapter objectives

By completing the work in this chapter, you should be able to:

- appreciate what makes a good central research question
- assess potential topics for your project
- understand the ethical considerations involved in research design.

Introduction

By now you will have at least a rough idea of what you are required to produce and how you can manage the process of producing a project. So far, most of what we have looked at can be applied to any project, so the time has come to start focusing on your project. The best place to start is by looking at how you can go about finding a good topic.

How should I go about choosing my topic?

Not with deciding to do questionnaires!

That may seem an odd thing for me to write, but you'd be surprised how often I've heard the phrase 'doing something with questionnaires' in early project discussions about topic.

Firstly, and hardly surprisingly, questionnaires are to do with your choice of method, not of topic. Choosing your topic and your CRQ will influence your choice of methodology, which will in turn inform your choice of method(s), which may be or may not be, as it turns out, questionnaires. In other words, deciding at the beginning to do questionnaires is jumping three steps ahead and then having to work backwards – seriously not recommended.

So, back to the first step then.

Your topic choice involves two elements: your choice from what are called business functions – in other words, marketing, finance, human resource management, strategy, etc. – and your choice of industry sector. You get the idea – it will certainly relate quite closely to the words that appear in the module titles of your degree programme. You need to consider your ability and your interest in the business function. Are you good at it? Do you enjoy studying it?

Time for self-reflection and honest self-assessment

Don't worry – your honest answers are safe in this book!

Rate yourself on scales of 0 to 10 as to how good you are at all the business functions I've listed below (10 is excellent). I've put in a 'write-in' option as your degree programme might cover more than the basic core. Then assess yourself on how attracted you to are each of them. The order I've listed them in is alphabetical and has no significance.

	Your strength	Appeal to you
Finance	....	....
HRM	....	....
Information Technology	....	....
Marketing	....	....
Operations Management/Logistics	....	....
Strategy	....	....
....	....	....

Be absolutely honest – if you are not, the only person you are deceiving is yourself, and you may well come to regret any self-deception.

Go back to the box on page 27 and make sure you have made an appropriate choice there!

In a perfect world you would have scored yourself, with ruthless honesty, 10 in every category. You wouldn't have got much further forward in choosing the business function element of your topic, but you would be able to relax in making the choice.

As it is just possible that you didn't score yourself so highly, how do you interpret your scores? First I would suggest you simply add the two scores for each business function together and jot the totals in the right-hand margin. In general, the higher the combined score, the better that business function will suit you as your choice. Anything where you have scored less than twelve, I would advise rejecting.

If you've got more than one business function with more or less the same total, I would push you gently towards the one with the higher score in 'Appeal to you'. Over time, as you become more and more involved in the work your project generates, you will build expertise in that business function, and any re-assessment at a later date will tend to be a higher score. On the other hand, because of the sheer amount of work involved, your natural interest in the business function may diminish, simply due to over-exposure. If you don't at least start with a very high score for 'Appeal', you may find the later stages of producing a project become a real chore – not a pleasant prospect, especially as having enough mental stamina may be the factor which will determine whether or not you complete.

The other element of your topic which you need to choose is the industry setting or, more specifically probably, a sub-sector within that sector. Examples of sector and sub-sector are transport and airlines, or leisure services and health spas. You may well choose to be even more specific and choose an individual company.

Here you can be guided by a combination of the following considerations:

- any inherent interest you have for whatever reason
- any previous experience in that sector/sub-sector that has given you interest
- any contacts you may have in that sector/sub-sector
- any intention you have of seeking employment in that sector/sub-sector.

A final factor might be how topical issues are in the particular sector/sub-sector. But be wary if your choice of sector/sub-sector is a 'hot topic' in the news. As this is part of the content of your project, you might want to think twice about choosing a topic that other people are likely to be choosing. Remember, your project is in part about assessing your ability to work independently, so set yourself up so that you do work independently. Also remember that today's 'hot topic' in the media will either soon grow cold, or, even worse, stay in the news because the situation is forever changing. Over recent years, I've come across students who, for fairly obvious reasons, namely, the coincidence of personal interest and 'hot topic', want to do a project on the finances of Liverpool or Manchester United. My advice has been invariably 'Forget it!' Even the person most indifferent to what is happening in football will, I guess, be aware that the issues of re-financing and debts come high on the agenda of these two clubs (and many other clubs of course). The amount of change in the last, say, two or three years has been phenomenal, and there is no reason to imagine that it won't continue right up to the hand-in date of your project; you'd be investigating and attempting to analyse, and please forgive the irresistible choice of metaphor, ever-changing goal posts.

The introduction of football as a topic raises another important point, at least with regard to those of you who are on degree programmes with titles relating to specific sectors or sub-sectors of industry – Sports Management, Tourism Management, Hospitality Management, Events Management, Creative Industries Management, etc. Degrees with this kind of name usually specify that your research project must be set within the area implied by the degree name. If you have any doubts – Leisure Management, for example, might be considered to have rather fluffy boundaries – check your choice of sector/sub-sector/company with your supervisor and/or your projects module leader. You don't want the person marking your project to be thinking, 'Great project, but not on this degree programme, so I'll have to give it a fail grade for not being what was asked for'. I can assure you from experience – this very occasionally does happen.

The two different elements of the topic – business function and industry sector – give you an opportunity to vary the scope of your research. For example, a project set in 'marketing' and 'telecommunications' offers an enormous scope – way too big, in fact, to be done justice in an undergraduate business project with its restriction on word length. On the other hand, 'intensive advertising campaigns in free local newspapers' and 'independent mobile telephone retailers in the Manchester area' have a much smaller scope. This gives you a handy way of 'opening up' or 'closing down' the topic to find the right scope – the scope which will suit the number of words you are restricted to. In practice, it is the industry sector/sub-sector/company which is the more useful in this respect; in general you will need to focus on a fairly tight group of theories within a specific part of your business function.

This process of 'opening up' or 'closing down' the scope of the topic has implications for the size of **population** of what you have chosen to look at, and hence on the **sample** size you will need to consider if using questionnaires or doing interviews. We'll come back to the issue of samples on page 84, but bear in mind that your choices at this stage – how far down the hierarchy of sector/sub-sector/company – may well restrict the research methods you can use. For example, small populations lend themselves to interviews whereas large populations do not. More on this later.

As we have seen, you need to think about the research paradigm you will be using. I suggest you think again about whether you are more comfortable working in words or in numbers.

Do you enjoy writing? Are you happy handling statistics?

If you answered 'Yes!' to both, that's the perfect pairing, and you will have freedom of choice in which paradigm you use.

Population

The total number in the group you are researching.

Sample

The group within the population you are measuring, from which you actually gather data.

If you answered 'No!' to both, you are in trouble! Start thinking which is the lesser of two evils so far as you are concerned – words or numbers.

If you answered 'Yes! and 'No!' once each, relax – you are like most people.

Perhaps another way of approaching this issue of research paradigm is to ask yourself which subjects you enjoyed and/or were better at when you were at school or college. Did you prefer subjects like history, English and art, or did you prefer maths, physics and information technology? You've probably guessed where I'm going with this one – history, English and art are examples of 'the arts', word-oriented subjects, whereas maths, physics and information technology are examples of 'the sciences', number-oriented subjects.

This is a good point at which to turn to the choice of your central research question as, perhaps surprisingly to you, what is known as the question word – the word which begins the question – can be strongly linked to your research paradigm, and hence to the research methods you will use. 'How much?' and 'To what extent?', for example, not only suggest number-driven approaches – they are gagging for them! Plain old 'How?' points more to words, however, especially if the answer is likely to be a complex one.

The exact formulation of your CRQ is not something that will come to you in a flash – you will start with a rough draft, and refine iteratively (remember that? – see page 14 if you don't). This iteration may well go through several phases before you get the right version. We've already seen above how you might want to open up or close down the scope of your project – so, for example, what starts as 'in the United Kingdom' in your CRQ may well change to 'in the London area', and then 'in Ealing'.

Talking of iteration and your CRQ is all very well, you cry, but how do I start the process? How do I go about getting my first draft of it?

There are two ways to make this first but vital step. They both involve inspiration, or rather techniques to improve your chances of inspiration.

1. *Brainstorm with fellow students*: Yes, I know the student project is all about working independently, but at this stage (but no further!) it can be very helpful to bounce ideas around with fellow students. The more you discuss your topic, the greater the chance that you will find something puzzling, and then you can formulate that into a question that needs to be answered by research – your research.
2. *Start searching the literature*: Remember that you have to identify a gap in the body of knowledge. As you trawl through the e-databases of academic journal articles, you may well start to see where there is a gap – something nobody has researched, and hence we don't know. This may well be in terms of 'Ah, we know about things in country or region X, or in industry/sub-sector/company Y, but not in the region or company that interests me'. In other words, you will find research that is relevant to the topic you have chosen, but which doesn't precisely cover it. Tease out the CRQs of these relevant articles, and see if you can tweak them to give you a similar CRQ, one which fits your topic and will make a contribution.

Do bear in mind that the role of the lecturer nominated to advise you individually, your supervisor, does not include producing a ready-made CRQ for you. The very first draft must come from you. He or she can then help you refine it.

First thoughts of my CRQ

Just to encourage you to take that magic step, jot down below your very first pre-draft draft of your CRQ. Go on, have a go – you can't put it off forever.

It *was* in the form of a question, wasn't it? Circle the 'question word(s)'. You'll need to go back and reword your 'question' if it turns out it isn't actually a question!

Once you've got that very first version, you can begin to assess its merits, and probably start the inevitable process of iterating – refining or tweaking it.

Now, there are several criteria we need to use in assessing the merits of a CRQ.

Answerable through research

Can you actually get an answer through research? Questions such as 'What is the purpose of living?' and 'Does heaven exist?' are jolly interesting, but not answerable through research.

Is it more a matter of opinion than of fact? An example here would be a question such as 'Is Microsoft a good company?' (which is also a bad CRQ because how on earth would we all agree a definition of what exactly a 'good' company is?).

In particular, research will only give you an informed guess about the future, so avoid speculation and crystal-ball-gazing. Any question beginning 'What does the future hold for …?' is not answerable by research even though it may lead to interesting and informed speculation.

Access

Will you be able to access the data you need? This may refer to pre-existing data – what is known as secondary data – or data that you will need to 'create', for example, through questionnaires, interviews or observation – what is known as primary data. You should be able to check pretty quickly whether or not the secondary data you need exists and is reliable, but it's a bit more complex with primary data. Here we are talking about access to people who will be your source of data. Depending on getting interviews with Board members of a company is not likely to happen (unless your friend or relative happens to be the Managing Director, that is), and even getting access to the general public can be problematic. For example, if your topic was in the travel industry, you might want to interview travellers or distribute questionnaires to them. You may well find, and will find if you are looking at talking to airline passengers at an airport, that you will be stopped from doing so by the relevant authorities. Even asking for permission will result in a polite refusal, on not unreasonable security grounds, but also on the grounds that they don't want their airport concourse full of students pestering their passengers. Consider whether seasonality might create issues of access – you are likely to have to collect data in winter (because of the timing of the academic year). Does this timing mean you will be more or less likely to find people you want to interview? Seasonality affects more business sectors than you might imagine – most have predictable busy and slack periods, so you are better off if you pick a sector which is slack when you plan to collect primary data.

The bleeding obvious

Just remember that no one actually makes it onto *Mastermind* answering questions on 'The Bleeding Obvious'. Research should always aim for at least a small element of surprise in its outcomes and conclusions.

Appropriateness to your degree

At most universities, if not all, there will be a requirement that undergraduate business projects are about business and management. It seems obvious enough and surely that won't create problems, will it? It doesn't generally, but from my experience there are ways in which you might just be tempted to stray a bit too far off centre. These are when you are drifting into sociology, in particular gender and race issues, or into psychology in the case of some areas of marketing and human resource management. If you have the slightest doubt, check with your supervisor and/or the module leader. In these cases you will generally be able to stick with your topic, but will need to revisit your CRQ.

> The question of appropriateness to your degree is particularly important if you are on a degree programme which includes the name of an industry sector in its title. To me, sports tourism is certainly acceptable as a topic for a Tourism Management degree, but rather less so for a Sports Management degree. Again, you need to check before you get too deeply into your project.

Scope

Even at this stage it may be clear that you are taking on way too big a task for an undergraduate business research project. The whole world is probably just a tad unrealistic in most cases, certainly if you are thinking of using questionnaires with the public.

Time for Reflective Exercise 2. Turn to page 147.

With the criteria above in mind, you will be asked to assess eight potential CRQs.

Right, I've got at least the first version of my central research question – isn't it a bit airy-fairy?

Well, that's rather hard for me to answer as I can't see what you've written! First attempts are usually just that – they need tweaking into an improved version. They fall into two categories. They are most often too airy-fairy in the sense that they are asking a question which is too broad to be answered within the scope of an undergraduate project. For example, let's say you asked, 'What kinds of marketing strategies do car manufacturers use?' This is a really huge question and you would never be able to answer it in the timescale you have forced upon you. You would need to think in terms of narrowing its focus. This could be done but not looking at all car manufacturers based in all countries. In other words, you could focus it into something more manageable by putting in limits, either geographical and/or by companies you choose to look at. You could also limit yourself to, for example, advertising in UK newspapers, which would make a great deal of sense as you are then researching competition in a particular market place. Always remember, *you* choose the question to ask.

At the other end of the scale, your central research question might be too specific, for example, 'What internet marketing strategies is the Morgan Motor Company using to promote its new 3-Wheeler?' Two problems arise in this scenario. Your research project has become a mini-project (sorry for the pun!) which you would be pushed to get a long enough write-up from, and probably it is not a complex enough issue to be worthy of an undergraduate project.

In the early stages of refining your central research question it is perfectly normal to find yourself 'opening up' or 'closing down' your topic to give yourself something workable. Bear in mind that someone writing a Masters dissertation or a PhD thesis will be facing similar issues, but finding different solutions – a dissertation or a thesis requires more complex issues and longer write-ups. These three – the undergraduate project, the Masters dissertation and the Doctoral thesis are similar in what is required of them but differ in complexity and length, so you need to hone your central research question to meet the complexity and length needs of the undergraduate project.

At this point it is appropriate to consider a very important issue that we have barely mentioned before – the issue of ethics – not least because problems may arise. Ethical issues need to be taken very seriously. Failing to do so could result in your project being rejected as failing to meet the Ethics Code provided by your university, and, since you are likely to be asked to get ethical approval for your project, it is vital that you take this on board at an early stage in designing your research project.

Can I just go ahead and ask anyone anything I need to?

In a word, no! If you are only planning to use secondary data, there will be no problems, but if you are planning to gather primary data through, for example, interviews, focus groups or questionnaires there may be problems. Groups of people for whom you will have difficulty in getting ethical approval include people under 18 years old. You are unlikely to get ethical approval if your method(s) of gathering data involve(s) deception. You will not be allowed to invade someone's privacy or access any confidential data held by someone else.

Write in below any restrictions your university's Code of Ethical Approval imposes

Why exactly do I need to think about ethics?

Codes of Ethics are there for a good reason – to protect the rights of other people, to ensure that you show respect to the people you are gathering data from, and to minimise the risks of putting yourself in danger or in trouble with the law.

You achieve this by submitting an application for ethical approval (the route to good ethics), and keeping good records of any approval you need to be allowed to collect data.

An excellent overview of how to apply ethical considerations in practice is given in the 5R model, as shown in Figure 4.1

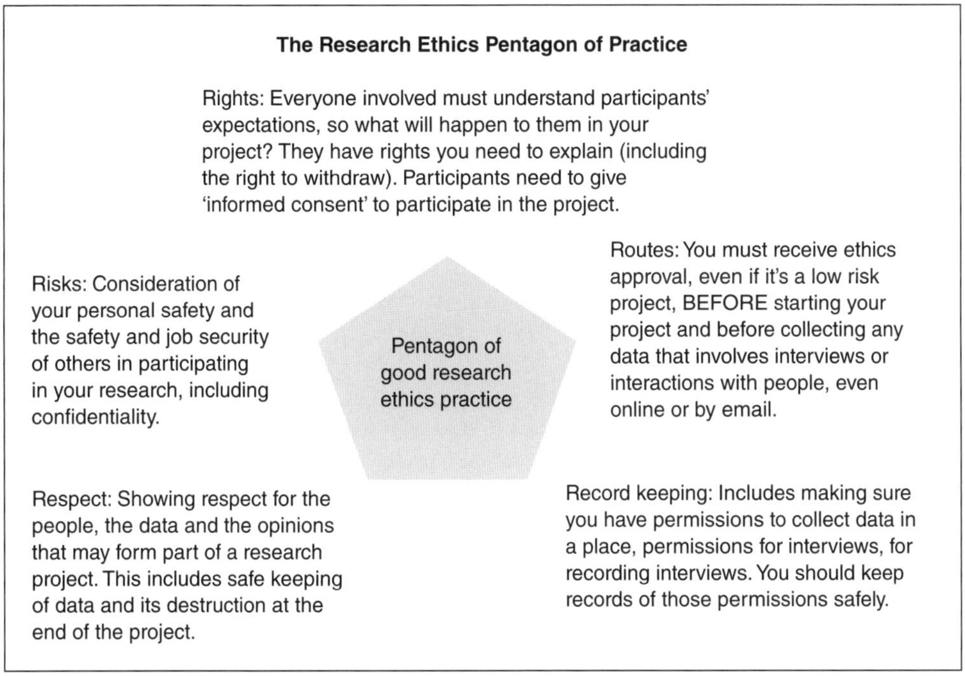

The Research Ethics Pentagon of Practice

Rights: Everyone involved must understand participants' expectations, so what will happen to them in your project? They have rights you need to explain (including the right to withdraw). Participants need to give 'informed consent' to participate in the project.

Risks: Consideration of your personal safety and the safety and job security of others in participating in your research, including confidentiality.

Routes: You must receive ethics approval, even if it's a low risk project, BEFORE starting your project and before collecting any data that involves interviews or interactions with people, even online or by email.

Pentagon of good research ethics practice

Respect: Showing respect for the people, the data and the opinions that may form part of a research project. This includes safe keeping of data and its destruction at the end of the project.

Record keeping: Includes making sure you have permissions to collect data in a place, permissions for interviews, for recording interviews. You should keep records of those permissions safely.

FIGURE 4.1   The research ethics pentagon of practice (de Nahlik and Marshall, 2009)

It is not difficult to design your research so that you avoid getting caught up in ethical issues. You simply avoid the problem areas, for example, by choosing not to interview those under 18.

Chapter conclusion

In this chapter we have covered the following key concepts:

- the topic of your research project, and how to go about choosing it
- the central research question, and the criteria for assessing its merits
- ethical considerations, and how they may affect what you can and can't do in researching for your project.

Again, as in previous chapters, stop and reflect on these topics. Use the above list as a kind of 'checklist of understanding' to see whether or not you are ready to go on to the next chapter – go back a few pages and follow the text again if you are still unclear on the basics of the concepts involved. You don't need to be 100 per cent confident in your understanding as we will be going over them again in a bit more depth.

Make sure you have reflected on each fill-in box, and that you have actually committed a response to paper.

5

Defining your Research Perspectives

Chapter objectives

By completing the work in this chapter, you should be able to:

- establish an appropriate research strategy
- understand how the two basic research perspectives are likely to lead to different strategies, different methodologies and different choices of research methods
- explain the basic components of the research process.

Introduction

We now need to delve a little deeper into the two research paradigms – positivist and phenomenological.

As human beings we tend to fall into one of two groups in the way we see the world and the way we interpret it. Which one of the two boxes in Table 5.1 do you identify with?

Most people tend to be more one than the other, although a few people are completely one rather than the other.

TABLE 5.1   Two ways of viewing the world

Box A	Box B
• You are more comfortable using numbers • You enjoy the sciences • You tend to judge things in a 'black or white' way • You believe the world consists of a set of absolute truths we can establish through research	• You are more comfortable using words • You enjoy the arts • You tend to judge things in terms of 'shades of grey' • You believe we all see the world as our own 'truth'

 Which one of the two boxes, A or B above, better describes you?

This all sounds a bit, well, philosophical, but it's real world business we're talking about, isn't it?

Indeed it is, but that's precisely why you need to think about this – you are thinking about how you see that real world, and that has important implications for your research design.

At a personal level, you are thinking about whether your approach is a hard scientific one or a softer arts one. We shall see shortly that different research designs are more appropriate for a scientific approach or an arts approach. It is therefore important that a) you use an appropriate design, and b) that design is one which you feel naturally comfortable with.

Let us go back for a moment to your central research question. Questions can be divided into two types. First there are those which lead to a 'yes' or 'no' answer. These take the grammatical form of a 'reversed statement':

Is Barclays the biggest bank in the UK?

Does BMW appeal more to older drivers?

On the other hand there are questions which begin with a 'question word' such as 'how', 'why', 'who', 'what', 'where', 'how many', 'how much'.

The first group of questions imply that there is a simple 'black' or 'white' answer, as do some of the 'question word' questions, such as 'who' or 'where'. On the other hand, questions which begin with 'how' or 'why' lead to more complex answers.

Robert Yin (2008) takes this argument a step further. He argues that different question words lead to different research strategies, and that these research strategies are appropriate to different circumstances (see Table 5.2).

TABLE 5.2   Relevant situations for different research strategies (Yin, 2008)

Strategy	Form of research question	Requires control over the behaviour of people being studied?	Focuses on contemporary events?
Experiment	how, why	yes	yes
Survey	who, what, where, how many, how much	no	yes
Archival analysis	who, what, where, how many, how much	no	yes/no
History	how, why	no	no
Case study	how, why	no	yes

The best research designs will check off against one, and only one, row in Table 5.2.

If you are still thinking about your central research question, start by looking at column 2, and then consider which research design, in column 1, is appropriate. For example, if your CRQ begins with 'how' or 'why' then using surveys, such as questionnaires, is going to be an inappropriate design.

Is the same true for interviews? Perhaps you were planning to interview senior people in a particular industry sector to answer a 'why' question. The reality is that the interview method in this case is actually going to answer a different question – 'What do senior people in the industry think is the reason that …'. This is of course a valid central research question, but it is not the same as finding out why something happens.

You should be far enough ahead in your planning to be able to check your plans against Table 5.2.

Do they check off against one row?

Epistemology

The study of knowledge. A good detailed explanation can be found at http://plato.stanford. edu/entries/ epistemology/.

To put this into a bigger picture we need to look very briefly at what is known as '**epistemology**', or, to put it in a more student-friendly way, 'the study of knowledge itself', which concerns answering questions like 'What is knowledge?' and 'What can we know and how?' You can relax though – we don't need to concern ourselves with actually answering questions like that! But we do need to concern ourselves with the implications of the answers to those questions.

By doing this we come to the two different research perspectives we looked at above. Remember the words we used to label these two perspectives or paradigms. The 'numbers', 'science', 'black or white answers' and 'one absolute set of truths' perspective is called 'positivism'. The other perspective – 'arts', 'words', 'shades of grey answers' and 'seeing our own truth' – is known by several names which you may come across – interpretivism, phenomenology and heuristics (which are slightly different in fact, but we don't need to worry about that!). I will use the term 'phenomenology' to be consistent.

It is this 'divide' between positivist approaches and phenomenological approaches that leads to different research methodologies and different research methods (see Figure 5.1).

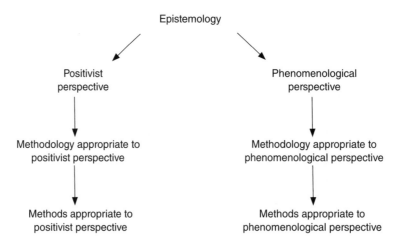

FIGURE 5.1   Different perspectives, different methodologies and different methods

The most obvious way in which the two different perspectives lead to different methods is in the two different kinds of research which you are probably already familiar with – a positivist perspective leads naturally to quantitative research methods (i.e. numerical data) and a phenomenological perspective leads naturally to qualitative research methods (i.e. word data).

The chances are that you will instinctively find yourself more willing to undertake qualitative research rather than quantitative research, or vice versa. So why did we need to go through all of this chapter so far? Simply because you need to be aware that consistency all the way through your research design is essential. The more consistent your research design, the better the outcomes will be.

Discussion of management as science or art

You may well have views on whether the study of management is a science or an art, and, indeed, whether management itself is a science or an art. My response to that is to say simply that you will see them as sciences if you tend by nature towards a positivist perspective, and as arts if you tend by nature towards a phenomenological perspective.

Discussion of disadvantages of mixing paradigms

It is generally considered to be bad practice to mix quantitative and qualitative methods, not least because to do so is to mix approaches from the two fundamentally different perspectives.

That said, I believe there are exceptions. For example, you might want to research how senior managers in a company view their products and investigate whether their view aligns with those of their customers. To research the views of senior managers it would be appropriate to use interviews (qualitative), but to get a sufficient size of sample on the views of their customers it would be appropriate to use quantitative questionnaires, where customers respond to statements by marking a 1 to 5 scale showing their level of agreement or disagreement with each statement. In short, the first phase of the research design uses interviews and the second phase uses questionnaires.

So, try not to mix quantitative and qualitative methods unless you have a good solid reason for incorporating both into your research design.

Two general overviews of the research process

The two general overviews we will be considering are a simplified model and then we will move on to a more detailed model that will serve as a template for your project.

First we will look at a simplified model (Figure 5.2).

The relatively straightforward flow down the centre of Figure 5.2, marked by the thick arrows, is the main thrust of the process. The thinner arrows, which mostly lead back to the first step, are just optional steps which you would only need to take if you had hit a snag and had to redesign the previous step(s) so as to avoid the snag.

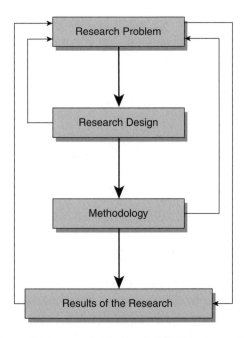

FIGURE 5.2   The outline of a research design (Allard-Poesi and Maréchal, 2001)

While this model is helpful as a simple overview, it lacks the detail which would be necessary for you use as a template in designing your research project. Our second model (Figure 5.3) is much more detailed and can be used as a template.

Take some time to work your way through Figure 5.3.

Again, strictly speaking, there should be additional optional arrows back to each of the previous levels in case you hit snags.

Here are some notes on Figure 5.3 which will help you to understand:

1. *Identify the broad topic of research interest*

    In some ways you may think this is the hardest stage, but it should be reasonably simple – you need to choose a topic which interests you, perhaps from an industry sector you would like to work in.

2. *Select the research focus/question and approach*

    Here you will be 'opening up' or 'closing down' the research topic to get the research required to an appropriate amount to fit into an undergraduate project. To help you in this, I would strongly recommend discussing your ideas with your project supervisor. At the same time, you should run your central research question past him/her.

1. **Identify the broad topic of research interest**

⇓

2. **Select the research focus/question and approach**

⇓

3. **Decide the design (methodology)**

How?   What about?   When?   Where?   From whom?

(Methods)   (Concerns)   (Timing)   (Site)   (Units)

Sampling?   ⇓   Operationalising?

4. **Prepare the instruments**
    Prepare the analysis

⇓

5. **Arrange the fieldwork; conduct a pilot**

⇓

6. **Collect the data**

⇓

7. **Organise the data**

Transcribe / Tabulate / Organise / Code

⇓

8. **Analyse**

Prepare the main features, relationships, patterns

⇓

9. **Interpret the results**

Draw out inferences, build up arguments

⇓

10. **Draw conclusions**

Relate your findings back to your research objectives,
your aims and your central research question

⇓

11. **Consider the implications**

FIGURE 5.3   A detailed overview of the research process (adapted from di Gregorio, 1996)

3. *Decide the design (methodology)*

    How will you gather your data?

    What about potential problems, such as getting access to people you want to interview?

    When will you need to gather your data? This is important in cases where there is a seasonal dimension, such as using tourists as your source of data. If you are from overseas and plan to gather data in your home country, will your holidays occur at the right time to fit in with your schedule to complete the project?

    Where do you plan to gather your data? Will you be allowed to gather data in that place? It's surprising how many places will not give you permission – so check this at an early stage in the process.

    From whom do you plan to gather data? This, your choice of 'unit of analysis', raises the issues of the size of the population of this set of people, and also the size your sample will need to be. See Chapter 8 for more on this.

    Sampling? How will you build your sample? Again, see Chapter 8 for more on this.

    Operationalising? How will you actually go about putting your research design into practice?

4. *Prepare the instruments*

    The instruments are the actual research tools you will use, that is, your specific questionnaire or set of questions for a series of structured interviews. Preparing how you will analyse the data you are planning to gather is really important at this stage – don't leave this until after you have actually gathered the data, or you may find that you have gathered either data in the wrong format, or even the wrong data.

5. *Arrange the fieldwork; conduct a pilot*

    Conducting a pilot – a dummy run, a test run at gathering data from a small number of people – is absolutely vital. It will show up, for example, any ambiguities in the questions you plan to ask – they will not be obvious to you; it's only other people who will see them!

6. *Collect the data*

    This is of course the central part, the focus, of the process, but it is perhaps surprising what a small part of the overall process it actually is.

7. *Organise the data*

    This involves sorting the data out and putting it into the format you will need for your analysis – transferring into an Excel spreadsheet, for example, which of course you will have prepared at step 4 above. You may need to 'code' it – this means putting general data, such as the transcripts of interviews, into predefined categories. It might, for example, involve assigning emotions, such as anger, disgust, contempt to what people are saying. You should not do the coding yourself. Rather, you should recruit at least a couple of mates to do this, and then you can chair a meeting of the coders to negotiate agreements where they have coded differently. In your write-up you will need to explain how coding took place.

8. *Analyse*

   We'll return to this in more detail in Chapter 9.

9. Interpret the results

   Your results will be, for example, in the form of statistical correlations. These will need to be interpreted – put back into meaningful English, being careful that you don't make more of the results than is justified.

10. *Draw conclusions*

    You need specifically to relate your findings back to your research objectives, and from these back to your aims, and finally back to your central research question – this, after all, is what your project is all about.

11. Consider the implications

    This is your chance to explain the significance of your research. You should also point out any limitations to how your research findings can be generalised, make any recommendations for the industry sector in which you've been researching, and suggest any interesting lines for further research.

Chapter conclusion

In this chapter we have covered the following key concepts:

- the consequences of selecting different research perspectives and, most importantly
- the design of a research project.

Before proceeding, go back and work your way through the 11 steps in Figure 5.3 again, and the notes that followed.

Section conclusion

That brings us to the end of Section 2, in which we have looked at the major topics that make up the research project and how you can put them into practice. Go back to page 23 and review the questions and outline answers in the Section Guide.

Once you have done that, complete the final 'Stop box' of Section 2 below. By doing this, you will begin to focus on your own individual research project.

Time to take stock!

Before you rush headlong into Section 3, you need to assess how much progress you have made. In particular, you need to assess where you have got to with your choice of topic by completing Table 5.3.

TABLE 5.3   Locating your *project*

Business function	Industry sector
Which function?	Which sector?
Which part of the function?	Which sub-sector?
Any particular areas of theory?	Any particular company or group of companies?

Recommended reading

Creswell, J.W. (2009) *Research Design: Qualitative, Quantitative, and Mixed Method Approaches* (3rd edn), Thousand Oaks: Sage.

SECTION 3

Producing Your Project

Section guide

Our work so far has been essentially preparatory – getting you to the starting line of actually producing a project if you like. This has of course involved a great deal of work on your part, and, you might argue, with not much to show for it. Do not be down-hearted. Imagine all the preparation Mo Farah has done before he steps up to the line to run a 10,000 metres race. Without all the preparation he has put in, there would be no chance of him winning. In other words, preparation is essential and time consuming, but without doing it thoroughly, you will not 'win' the race to actually produce a completed project.

So, it's to actually getting down to producing a project that we now turn.

Here in Section 3 you will be looking at how to:

- do your literature review (Chapter 6)
- put your methodology into practice (Chapter 7)
- select the appropriate research methods for your project (Chapter 8).

 Stop and go back to Figure 5.3.

Remind yourself of the various steps in the research process. Note how it falls into two phases – the steps before the gathering of data and the steps after the gathering of data.

Section 2 has supported you through steps 1 and 2. Section 3 focuses on steps 3, 4 and 5 (before you gather data), and Section 4 will focus on steps 7 onwards (after you gather data).

From this point on, the process you share with other students will start to become more distinct and more specific to your project. This is inter-connected with the fact that the content of your project is becoming more significant in your work (check back to page 30 to see the shifting balance between process and content).

 Recommended reading

Cassell, C. and Symon, S. (2004) *Essential Guide to Qualitative Methods in Organizational Research*, London: Sage.

Gummesson, E.G. (2000) *Qualitative Methods in Management Research* (2nd edn), Thousand Oaks: Sage.

Maykut, P. and Morehouse, R. (1994) *Beginning Qualitative Research*, London: Falmer.

6

Doing your Literature Review

Chapter objectives

By completing the work in this chapter, you should be able to:

- understand why a literature review is necessary
- appreciate that a literature review adds value to a literature search
- explain how research fills mapped gaps in knowledge in order to make a contribution
- structure your literature review
- understand the need for systematically recording references as you conduct your research.

Introduction

You will have certainly already conducted a literature search many times during your studies. This may have been as basic as putting a key word into Google, or, more productively, exploring the online academic databases of journal articles your university provides. If the latter are not familiar to you, head straight over to your university library and ask them to show you how to access these databases.

In this chapter I will be assuming that you have found access to these databases and are therefore in a position to start on a literature search and thence conduct a literature review.

Why do I need to do a literature review?

Your literature review should contain two elements:

1. a review of the research that has already been conducted in the field which you are researching
2. a review of the relevant theoretical frameworks.

Obviously there may well be areas of overlap, but too many would suggest that there is little new to discover and you may be better off looking at something at least slightly different.

Your review of research already conducted in the field contextualises your proposed contribution.

You look at relevant theoretical frameworks because you will need to use them for analysis and synthesis. Their use is a major plank in your case that what you have done is valid.

Your literature review needs to be discursive – in other words, 'telling a story' that leads to a clear conclusion – with respect to your project, not simply descriptive. In other words, you need to develop a logical argument that leads the reader forward to your methodology and methods chapters.

This chapter of your project is a literature review, not merely the output of a literature search – you need to 'add value'. You add value by critiquing – commenting on both negative and positive aspects of – what you find in your initial search. This involves explaining how your planned research fits in as a missing piece in an existing jigsaw puzzle. For example, if you wanted to research football club finance, you may well find that your particular central research question has been asked, and answered, with respect to the biggest clubs in the Premier League, but that no one so far has researched a club in the rather different financial world of League 2 or even the Football Conference. Critiquing also includes pointing out how your research may be similar to pre-existing research but is different in some vital way. For example, you may find that your topic has been researched thoroughly by American academics, researching American companies, but so far it has not been researched deeply in UK contexts. This example might be thought of as showing a relatively minor difference, but in areas such as marketing and human resource management there may be quite large difference between American and UK customers and employees.

How to set the context, make the topic sound interesting and identify why the research is worthwhile

There are two starting points for your literature review: looking for literature relevant to your industry sector, and looking for literature on your choice of business function (e.g. marketing).

With luck, your lectures in other modules will have given you some ideas. If you are really starting from scratch, there are two good sources:

1. The electronic databases of academic articles provided by your university library. A typical example, which most universities subscribe to, is Ebsco. Other examples include databases provided by the publishers of journals such as Sage, Wiley, Routledge, Pearson. You will of course be confined to the databases which your particular university subscribes to. If your study programme hasn't included sessions on how to use these databases, I would strongly recommend that you find out about using them from your subject librarian. One particular advantage of using articles from these databases is that you can download the articles as .pdf files, which allows you to re-read them as required.
2. Google Scholar (http://scholar.google.co.uk/, then untick the 'patents' box).

There is no doubt in my mind that the first of these will be the better source. This is because it includes sources for which your university will have paid a subscription whereas Google Scholar will only allow you access to the more restricted range of free articles.

Searching with search engines

Using too broad a term in a search engine will produce too many results, and using too narrow a term will produce too few. You need to develop a strategy for searching. Although your search is specific to you, there are some general guidelines available for developing your individual strategy – for example see www.lib.berkeley.edu/TeachingLib/Guides/Internet/Strategies.html.

Your university library will be able to help you in developing your online research strategy, and the people there will have a good knowledge of relevant specialist resources.

Stop and write in appropriate terms for you to search with:

Business function:

Industry sector:

Mapping the gap in knowledge to make a contribution (but probably not a lot!)

Your literature review is essentially a mapping exercise. You're setting out the limits of the gap in knowledge which you plan to fill – not by mapping the gap itself, but rather by mapping, and explaining, what lies around the gap.

Once you have identified your gap in knowledge, stop and reflect on what the reasons might be for the gap still existing. It may be that there is a major barrier to doing research in this area, such as the extreme difficulty in gathering data. Make sure, as far as it is possible, that you will not face any such barrier.

References

The references which you include at the end of your research project is a list of books, journal articles, websites, etc., which are cited in the main text. It does not include resources which you consulted but have not cited.

One useful technique for building up the number of articles to include is to work forward from relevant articles you find to articles listed in the **references** of such articles. By definition they will have some relevance, although it is for you to judge just how much relevance.

The deeper you get into the work, the clearer the gap in knowledge should become. You will start to get some idea of the size of the gap, and you will very likely want to tweak your central research question to 'open up' or 'close down' the gap. This is perfectly normal as you can't have any real sense of the size of the gap until you actually do the literature review.

Structuring your literature review

The process of conducting your literature search may be confusing and frustrating if you start to find too many useful and appropriate articles. We have seen how you open up and close down your topic in the light of this. But the question remains of how you can put together the articles which remain after any opening up or closing down.

The best approach to take is to group them around themes.

Let's take as an example the central research question, 'What do UK and Irish airline executives perceive as the causes of "success" and "failure" in their industry sector, and to what do they attribute success?'

In order to answer this question, it is first necessary to establish how these executives define 'success' and 'failure'.

Three academic areas emerge as themes for this research as we proceed with an initially unfocused literature search, each with its own literature and frameworks, and these are listed in Table 6.1.

TABLE 6.1   Example of literature review themes

General	Specific
Strategy	Success and failure; development of organisations
Organisational behaviour	Causal attribution
Industry context	Airline

We can thus begin to map these three themes, in particular looking at where they overlap. This leads us to a schema such as the one shown in Figure 6.1.

FIGURE 6.1   Example of mapping research themes

The strategy and the organisational behaviour themes overlap to some extent in organisational theory, while strategy and the specific industry context also overlap.

Organisational behaviour and the airline industry overlap to some extent in the area of human factors – that is, cockpit systems and flight deck management – but this highly specific overlap is of no relevance to the particular central research question ('What do UK and Irish airline executives perceive as the causes "success" and "failure" in their industry sector, and to what do they attribute "success"?') and is shown in italics in the mapping.

The intention of the research is to provide a contribution at the overlap of the three areas:

- Strategy: to contribute to the knowledge of what practising strategists perceive as 'success' and 'failure'.
- Organisational behaviour: to contribute to the knowledge of causal attribution.
- Airline industry: to contribute to the knowledge by exploring at the individual level from a phenomenological perspective rather than from the conventional economic perspective of the organisational and industry levels.

Strategy, it emerged in the literature search, has been linked with each of the other areas previously, but a new research project could explore the three-way overlap – in Figure 6.1, the all-important empty gap in the very middle – by looking at 'success', 'failure' and the perceived causes of 'success' in the airline industry.

As you progress with your literature research jot down here the key words from articles you find. Look to group them into three or so themes.

On a larger sheet of paper, start to map them so as to show a gap in knowledge which your project can fill.

Recording literature you find

Nothing can be more frustrating than, in the final week before you have to hand in your finished project, discovering that you have failed to record the precise source of an article or book chapter that you need to include in your project's bibliography, with appropriate citation in the main text. It is essential that you keep a full record of everything that you read during your literature search which might be at all likely to prove useful to your project. In the bad old days this might have been bulky and unmanageable card-index filing systems. Today, thank goodness, we have specialist software, such as EndNote, ProCite, Reference Manager and RefWorks.

Most of these packages have features which are particularly useful for doing your project. These include:

- A 'cite as you write' facility. With this switched on, you can type in a Word document, select the item you wish to cite from the bibliographical database you have previously created, and then with a single click you can insert not only the citation in your text but also the full reference in the bibliography, in its right place alphabetically, at the end of your project.
- The ability to set the style of referencing you want. For business projects this is normally the Harvard style of referencing, but make sure you use the one prescribed in your project module handbook.
- A facility to import references from the internet. For example, you might have found a number of articles using the search term 'car manufacturer Korea'. You will then be able to import them in bulk into your bibliographical database.
- A section in each entry where you can paste short passages of the article which you may want to quote in your project.

Each entry in your database will have the option for you to enter a key word or words. If you do this systematically, you will find searching at a later date much easier.

Check out which software package your university provides for building up your own personal bibliographical database. Also find out what handouts there are to help you in learning how to use the software. Get them and use them!

It may take a little time to get used to the bibliographical software but it is definitely worth the effort. Not only does it pay dividends when you get to the writing-up phase of your project, but also you can use the software when writing essays for assessment in other modules.

A small caution!

Unlike other referencing systems, Harvard is subject to local variations. Essentially these consist of matters such as whether journal titles should be italicised or underlined. Choose one variant and stick to it – as long as you are consistent, there will be no problem.

If you really can't hack either bibliographical database software or the Harvard system of referencing, the last desperate alternative is an online reference generator such as the one available at www.citethisforme.com/.

Why is it necessary to reference your project anyway?

As we noted above, the objective of the literature review is to identify any previous research in your area, and to identify theoretical frameworks you will use in your analysis. In any case, as research work, it is necessary to have an audit trail – the reader needs to be given directions to your sources should they want to access those sources themselves. This allows you to validate claims you make.

Again, like using bibliographical software, you will need to develop the appropriate micro-skills. Here too your university library will have handouts, normally available through your university intranet, showing you how to write the reference of every conceivable source, from book chapters, through journal articles, to websites. If you are working from a journal article which is available online, you should reference it as if you were reading the journal as print copy.

All references should be given in one single list at the end of the project, not different sections for different kinds of sources, or on a chapter-by-chapter basis – and should be in alphabetical order of author. The list is unnumbered and unbulleted.

Referencing systems

The system for referencing generally accepted by business schools is the Harvard system. All sources are listed in one bibliography (references), and reference is made to them by bracketing the author's family name plus year of publication plus page number in the text (citations). See the page on citation and referencing (page 128) for an example of a citation in text.

A second reason why you have to use a standard citation and referencing system is to protect yourself from any accusation of plagiarism, but we will explore the issue of plagiarism later.

Chapter conclusion

In this chapter we have covered the following key concepts:

- how the literature review involves adding value to a literature search
- defining a gap in knowledge and hence identifying the contribution you plan to make with your research project
- citing and referencing.

As in previous chapters, stop and reflect on these topics. Use the above list as a kind of 'checklist of understanding' to see whether or not you are ready to go on to the next chapter – go back a few pages and follow the text again if you are still unclear on the basics of the concepts involved. Unlike with previous chapters, this time you need to be reasonably confident in your understanding as we will not be going over them again.

Make sure you have reflected on each fill-in box, and that you have actually committed a response to paper.

Recommended reading

Hart, C. (1998) *Doing a Literature Review*, Thousand Oaks: Sage.

Machi, L.A. and McEvoy, B.T. (2009) *The Literature Review*, Thousand Oaks: Corwin.

Ridley, D. (2012) *The Literature Review: A Step-by-Step Guide for Students* (2nd edn), London: Sage.

7

Methodology into Practice

Chapter objectives

By completing the work in this chapter, you should be able to:

- plan out your research by devising a central research question, some aims and some research objectives
- identify (and hence minimise) potential problems such as access to interviewees, data availability, time costs, financial costs and seasonality
- calculate the size of a sample needed for a given population
- choose between gathering primary data and using secondary data
- assess the quality of secondary data
- explain the concepts of reliability and validity
- understand issues of bias and how to minimise them.

Introduction

This chapter takes us to the very heart of the process of producing your research project – how to design your programme of research work and produce a realistic and workable methodology.

How do I plan out my research?

We have already seen that the core of the research design and its structure consist of a hierarchy of three layers:

- a central research question
- aims
- research objectives.

Your central research question does need a touch, but only a touch, of airy-fairyness in that there should not be an obvious answer to it. Nor should the way you are going to answer it be too obvious at first sight.

The way to remove excess airy-fairyness and give some insight into your research strategy is to set up a hierarchy or pyramid of investigation. Overarching everything you do is the central research question. From this, we establish two or three aims, and from each of these we derive two or three research objectives. The easiest way to see how each of these three – the central research question, the aims and the research objectives – are inter-connected levels of the same research process is by looking at a couple of examples. The following, in Table 7.1, are just two examples, untried and unproven (and possibly unworkable!), but they serve to explain how the three concepts are related. They are just examples – they are not blueprints and should therefore not be used as blueprints.

TABLE 7.1   Breaking a central research question down into aims and research objectives

	Sport Management example	Tourism Management example
Central research question	Does playing in the Premiership have a significant impact on a club's financial performance?	Is there a link between perceived success and actual performance of UK airlines?
Aims	1. To identify three clubs: one that has played steadily but unspectacularly in the Premiership; one that has moved in and out a number of times; and one that has played regularly but unspectacularly in the second flight. 2. To identify significant financial and non-financial measures of their success.	1. To establish measures of perceived success of UK airlines. 2. To establish measures of actual performance of UK airlines. 3. To examine any relationship between them.
Research objectives	1. To establish profit (or loss) data and revenues for Everton, Leicester City and Sheffield United for the last five years. 2. To establish specific non-financial measures such as mean position and end-of-season position in their respective leagues. 3. To establish statistically which factors have the greatest correlation with profit over the last five years.	1. To find through questionnaires which UK airlines members of the public see as successful. 2. To analyse civil aviation data on airline performance. 3. To test their relationship using coefficients of correlation.

Breaking down a CRQ into aims, and aims into research objectives

The aims and objectives flow from the central research question via the methodology to the research you undertake. They are the key to developing a sense of logical flow in what you do, and in building the case that your conclusion(s) are unarguable. They form a hierarchy of logic and its application.

Central research question

The central research question is essentially conceptual. It does not necessarily give an indication of how it will be answered. It identifies the gap in knowledge you will fill and hence make a contribution.

Your project will have one central research question.

Aims

Aims are a mix of the conceptual and the practical. They begin to move the central research question towards the specific research you plan to undertake. They break the central research question into perhaps two, or at most three, lines of investigation, with probably a hint of how you will proceed.

Research objectives

Research objectives develop each aim further, into perhaps two or three specific research objectives, translatable into real world research or, in other words, operationalisable in a relatively obvious way.

Note that you need research objectives and not personal objectives (and similarly you should have research aims rather than personal aims). For example, 'to understand' or 'to learn about' are personal processes – they relate to your own self-improvement rather than filling a gap in the broader body of knowledge. That doesn't make them bad aims or objectives for you personally; it means though that they are irrelevant as aims or objectives from a research point of view.

Significant though the differences are between personal and research objectives, in forming and refining your research objectives, it is helpful to use the SMART model for objectives. This model sets out that objectives should be:

- specific
- measurable
- achievable
- relevant
- time bound.

In the case of 'time bound' we are asking whether the objective can be achieved within the timescale set by the hand-in date of your project. You should use this list as a checklist for evaluating the quality of your chosen research objectives.

Go back and think about how these explanations of the three levels can be related to the two examples in Table 7.1.

Think about how your proposed central research question relates to these levels:

1. Is it really a central research question, or is it perhaps more appropriate as an aim of a wider CRQ?
2. Can you see how you can break *your* CRQ down into two or three aims?
3. Do these aims potentially offer workable research objectives?
4. Is the data to achieve these research objectives already available, or will you able to gather it?

This, and the boxes that follow, are probably the most important exercises in this book. The better you complete them, the better your finished project will be.

 (I recommend you photocopy this page before writing on it – you may well want to come back and revise your thoughts as you get deeper into your project.)

Proposed central research question

Proposed aims

1.

2.

3.

Proposed research objectives for aim 1

1.

2.

3.

(Continued)

(Continued)

Proposed research objectives for aim 2

1.

2.

3.

Proposed research objectives for aim 3 (if applicable)

1.

2.

3.

To see how well you have chosen, apply the following questions:

1. Does each page fit in with the descriptions of the three levels given above?
2. Are the research objectives precise in what they set out to achieve?
3. Are the research objectives achievable?
4. Is there a logical cascade from one level to the next?

If you don't answer 'yes' to any of these, go back and tweak your proposals so that they do!

Spend some time getting all this to fit together in a logical and coherent way. Do not proceed to the next section until you are satisfied with what you are proposing. Remember, it may be possible to tweak your proposals as you progress further into your project, but the further on in time you get the smaller the tweaks can be.

We have mentioned 'complexity' as an issue in all of this. But do you know whether what you are proposing is sufficiently complex, or, to put it another way, demanding enough?

To help you decide this, consider where the verbs you use in your CRQ, aims and research objectives fall within something known as Bloom's taxonomy (see Table 7.2). This classification of verbs that show progressively more complex levels of educational activity, with respect to learning outcomes, was first drawn up by a group of American education experts chaired by Benjamin Bloom in 1956. Since then it has been variously expanded and adapted.

TABLE 7.2 Bloom's taxonomy (developed from Bloom et al., 1956)

Six levels of complexity in behaviour		
1. Knowledge: The simple recall of information		
Arrange	Define	Describe
Label	List	Match
Name	Order	Recall
Recite	Recognise	Record
Relate	Repeat	Reproduce
State	Underline	
2. Comprehension: The interpretation of knowledge		
Arrange	Classify	Describe
Discuss	Explain	Express
Extrapolate	Identify	Indicate
Interpret	Locate	Report
Restate	Sort	Translate

(Continued)

TABLE 7.2 (Continued)

Six levels of complexity in behaviour		
3. Application: The application of knowledge to a new situation		
Apply	Choose	Demonstrate
Illustrate	Measure	Operate
Practise	Prepare	Schedule
Sketch	Solve	Use
4. Analysis: The breaking-down of knowledge into parts and the demonstration of relationships between these parts		
Analyse	Appraise	Calculate
Categorise	Compare	Contrast
Criticise	Differentiate	Discriminate
Distinguish	Examine	Experiment
Question	Test	
5. Synthesis: The bringing together of elements of knowledge to form a whole, and the building of relationships for new situations		
Arrange	Assemble	Collect
Compose	Conduct	Construct
Create	Design	Formulate
Manage	Modify	Organise
Plan	Prepare	Propose
Set up	Synthesise	Write
6. Evaluation: The making of judgements about the value of material and methods for given purposes		
Appraise	Argue	Assess
Attack	Compare	Defend
Estimate	Evaluate	Judge
Predict	Rate	Score
Select	Support	Value

This is a classification of many of the kinds of verbs that will arise in your aims and research objectives. Bloom argues that they fall into six levels of complexity with respect to behaviour. Applied to undergraduate studies, his Levels 1 and 2 equate to Year 1, his Levels 3 and 4 equate to Year 2, and his Levels 5 and 6 equate to the Final Year, and hence to the project.

You should therefore be working mainly with aims and objectives which have verbs at Bloom's Level 5 and 6 (see Table 7.2). This does not mean that you can't use verbs from Levels 1 to 4, just that at the critical point in your logical flow they must be from Levels 5 and 6.

It might interest you to know that lecturers use Bloom's taxonomy when writing exam questions and module descriptors. In this way they make sure that there is a progression as you move through the three taught years of your degree programme.

The more effort you put into planning your central research question, the aims, and the research objectives, the smoother actually producing your project will be. But just how perfectly can anyone plan?

Can I be sure it will pan out as I planned it?

A very simple answer – No! You need to realise at an early stage that the research process is never smooth. It is perfectly normal to hit a range of snags as you proceed, but you can plan ahead by trying to foresee the snags, and develop a Plan B in each case.

Let's consider some of the most common snags.

Access problems

Never assume that managers in companies will be willing to give up their valuable time to answer questions from an undergraduate student. After all, from their perspective, why should they? They may well see it as unfair to agree to see you if they don't agree to see every student who approaches them. If they are a senior person in a well-known organisation the number of requests they receive may run into thousands every year. I'm thinking here of companies like Ryanair, Virgin or Manchester United. Some companies in this position (Virgin is a good example) have produced information packs to send to students who approach them. Helpful though the intention is, there are a number of drawbacks from your perspective:

- You only get the information that they choose to give you. This may be skewed towards the 'good news', and it is unlikely that by good chance it is the precise data you need.
- The data may be skewed towards particular business functions, for example, towards finance or marketing. Great if that's what you've chosen to look at, but not exactly helpful if you want to research an HRM topic!
- Every other student who approaches them, this year and in previous years, will get precisely the same set of data. This makes it particularly difficult for you to fill a gap in knowledge.

Data availability and potential availability

If you've been systematic with your research design, you will have identified a precise requirement for data to analyse. Your first thoughts must then be, 'Does this data already exist, and, if so, is it available publicly?' As well as company websites it is worth checking whether the data is available from, for example, professional association websites or even government websites. An amazing example of the latter is the data (both operational and financial) collected annually by the Civil Aviation Authority on airlines and airports (www.caa.co.uk/default.aspx?catid=80&pagetype=90).

If the data you need is not available, you will either have to tease it out from the relevant company – the chances are that they will not be willing to give it to you as they will consider it 'commercially sensitive' – or you will actually have to generate it yourself. The latter option will lead you more naturally to researching customers rather than providers, simply on the grounds that customers are far more willing to give their thoughts than companies are to give you data.

This raises possible snags in how you might access customers. We have already noted that you will not be allowed to interview passengers at an airport, and, in general, you are unlikely to get permission to interview customers in any premises where they are buying goods and services. Not all public spaces are as public as they seem – shopping malls are normally private land, and you would need permission to interview there. The key point is that you will have to think through the practicalities of gathering data – don't assume there is a helpful world out there which can't wait to help you with your project.

Time costs

You should also think through very carefully the practicalities of gathering your data in terms of how much time it is going to take you. In the case of, say, questionnaires, you need to think of the time involved in the various stages of the process:

- designing the questions
- producing a print-ready copy of them
- photocopying them
- travelling to where you are going to use them
- finding a sufficient number of people willing to answer them (will one visit to your chosen location be enough?)
- transferring the results to your pre-prepared database for statistical analysis.

Financial costs

Rather like the time costs you need to plan this very carefully allowing for each cost. If we take postal questionnaires as an example, costs will include:

- printing them
- envelopes to send them out in
- postage stamps.

If you want to speculate on improving your hit rate (the percentage which are actually completed and returned to you), you may consider, at extra cost, including stamped self-addressed envelopes.

All of these costs suddenly become big when you multiply the unit cost by the number of questionnaires.

Seasonality

The timing of your project is largely shaped by the timing of the academic year and the hand-in date. The chances are that you will find yourself gathering data in the winter months, especially around Christmas and New Year. You need to stop and think whether this has implications. Obvious areas where this can be problematic are the travel and tourism industry and in professional sports, but it has more subtle implications in a wide range of industries if you are targeting consumers. You only have to look round the shops to realise how seasonal consumption is. I say this from the experience of trying to buy my wife a garden hammock for Christmas – not an easy undertaking!

Stop and write in possible snags with gathering data for your project.

1. Access problems

2. Data availability and potential availability

3. Time costs

4. Financial costs

5. Seasonality

Unless you have left the five spaces above empty, how are you going to overcome these snags? This may involve practical ways of overcoming them, or it may be necessary to rethink your design so that you have more snag-free data requirements.

The matter of sample size

In the paragraph above on 'Data availability and potential availability' we touched on the question of whether you are gathering data from companies or their customers. It's important to realise that these two different sources of data tend to lead to rather different kinds of data, and hence to rather different outcomes.

'Hard' data from a company, whether financial or operational, provides a source of information which will allow you to assess a company's performance. If, on the other hand, you gather data from the company's customers, you will have gathered data on the customers' perception of performance.

To put it another way, financial and operational data will help you to answer a CRQ such as 'How well is this company performing?' Data from customers will enable you to answer a subtly different question: 'How well is the company seen to be performing?' Tweaking your CRQ from one like the first to one like the second may remove a serious snag from the design of your research gathering, but it has resulted in rather more than just a change in emphasis. What you have changed is the unit of analysis and this has a major implication for your research design.

The unit of analysis is the individual 'item' (usually in fact 'person', if we are looking at a design involving interviews and/or questionnaires). The total number of possible choices of 'unit of analysis' is the population which you are researching.

Let me give you an example from my own research. For my PhD I investigated UK airlines. Looking at the airlines themselves led to a population of, at the time I did the research, 53 airlines.

I also surveyed, through interviews and questionnaires, members of the board of directors of these airlines – there were 353 at the time of my research.

If I had chosen to survey middle managers rather than directors, there would have been a much larger population. If I had chosen to survey the passengers of these airlines, the population would have been enormous, and in fact very difficult to put a number on.

Changing your unit of analysis changes the size of the population you are investigating. Why does this matter? It matters because the size of the population you are investigating determines the number you need to survey. Obviously the bigger the size of the population, the bigger your sample size needs to be. This issue of 'sample size' is a vital one. If your sample is too small, you cannot be confident in the results you come up with. Equally, surveying more people than is necessary is a waste of effort, time and money.

We need then to look carefully at the question of how many people you need to include in your survey results.

How big does my sample have to be?

The research problem: you want to find out something interesting about a group of people. For example, you want to know the proportion of young people (aged between

18 and 30) who have tried a particular brand of cola. It would not be practical, or cost effective, to ask everyone in that age group (called 'the population'). However, you can ask some of the people in that age group (called 'the sample'). That is, you can take a sample of the entire population to get an estimate of the proportion of young people who have tried your cola. As it is only an estimate, you will need to think about how confident you can be in the accuracy of that estimate.

Suppose you randomly selected a sample of a thousand people from the population, surveyed the sample with a questionnaire, and found out that 30 per cent had tried your cola. Would you expect that a different random sample of a thousand people from the same population would produce exactly the same result (30 per cent)? Intuitively, we would expect about the same percentage, but not exactly the same.

The first number you need to know is the size of the population you are taking the sample from. Let us call that P. We will call the sample size n. Now, some terminology I'm afraid, although it's not actually very difficult to understand!

The **confidence interval** (CI) is the plus-or-minus figure usually reported in newspaper or television opinion poll results (e.g. 30% ± 2% of British people believe that badgers are generally overweight). If you use a confidence interval of 4 per cent, and 47 per cent of your sample picks an answer, you can be 'sure' that, if you had asked the question of the entire relevant population, then between 43 per cent (47 − 4) and 51 per cent (47 + 4) of the population would have picked that answer. The sample is an estimate of the overall population.

The **confidence level** (CL) tells you how sure you can be that the result for the whole population sits within the sample interval. It is expressed as a percentage and represents the confidence of the 'real' result being within the confidence interval shown by the sample. The 95 per cent confidence level means you can be 95 per cent certain that the result for the population sits within the confidence interval; the 99 per cent confidence level means you can be 99 per cent certain. Most researchers use the 95 per cent confidence level (the choice of 95 per cent is merely a convention widely accepted by academic researchers; there is no inherent mathematical significance in the choice of number).

When you put the confidence level and the confidence interval together, you can say that you are 95 per cent confident that the true percentage for the population is between 43 per cent and 51 per cent.

The wider the confidence interval you are willing to accept, the more certain you can be that the whole population's answers would be within that range. For example, if you asked a sample of 1,000 people in a city which brand of cola they preferred, and 60 per cent said Brand A, you can be very certain that between 40 and 80 per cent of all the people in the city actually do prefer that brand, but you cannot be so sure that between 59 and 61 per cent of the people in the city prefer the brand.

I have developed the definitions above from a very useful website (www.surveysystem. com/sscalc.htm#terminology). You will see just how useful that website is very shortly as

Confidence interval

A measure of the accuracy of a survey, normally expressed as a plus-or-minus figure.

Confidence level

An estimate of how well the sample taken in a survey actually reflects the whole population. By convention, researchers normally seek a 95 per cent confidence level.

you can use a very nifty calculator they have developed to take all the pain out of having to do a load of statistics yourself!

So, P is already determined by your choice of population, and the CL is set, by convention, at 95 per cent.

If we say that, in order for your project to be credible in terms of showing that you have conducted the research process satisfactorily, your sample size n must be at least 50, then for any size of population we can calculate the confidence interval at a confidence level of 95 per cent.

Using the calculator at www.surveysystem.com/sscalc.htm (and assuming that 50 per cent of people respond with a yes to a yes/no question) we can draw up the following table:

TABLE 7.3   Population and sample size implications

Population (P)	Sample size (n)	Confidence level (CL)	Confidence interval (CI)
50	50	95%	0
75	50	95%	8
100	50	95%	9.8
300	50	95%	12.6
500	50	95%	13.1
1,000	50	95%	13.5
5,000	50	95%	13.8
60,000,000	50	95%	13.9

What exactly does that tell us?

If we had asked a question that had two possible responses, A or B, and we had found that the responses across the sample showed that 50 per cent of respondents had gone for A while obviously 50 per cent had gone for B, then:

- If the population had been 75, we can say with 95 per cent confidence that the population's responses would have been between 42 per cent (50 − 8) and 58 per cent (50 + 8).
- On the other hand, if the population had been 60,000,000 (e.g. people in the UK), we can say with 95 per cent confidence that the population's responses would have been between 36 per cent (50 − 13.9) and 64 per cent (50 + 13.9).

The first example would be fine for your project, but the second wouldn't – the possible range of actual responses is between 36 per cent and 64 per cent, or roughly between one third and two thirds would actually choose A (or, indeed B). Not really meaningful results!

Perhaps the question should not be 'How many in the sample?', the answer in terms of an undergraduate project being 50, but rather 'What is a suitable size of population from which to take a sample of 50?'

The answer to that is down to your judgement – what is an acceptable band for the whole of your chosen population?

Remember, at the design stage you can tweak the size of your chosen population by, for example, widening or narrowing your geographical scope.

What happens if there is only a small population?

Let us imagine that by tweaking your central research question you have identified a population which is exactly the magic '50'. First of all, you can forget any talk of confidence levels and so on – you survey the entire population and can then speak with total confidence!

But can you? If you sent your questionnaire to every person in that population of 50, could you reasonably expect all of them to reply? You would be very naïve if you did! The percentage who actually reply is called the response rate. It will depend on factors such as how long the questionnaire will take to fill in, how interested the people are in your research, how busy they are, how they are feeling – most of which are factors beyond your control.

It will also depend on how you administer the questionnaire – by post, by telephone or by personal contact. Never be over-confident in your expectations of response rate – 10 per cent is not unheard of for a boring, long questionnaire.

So, apart from tweaking your central research question geographically, is there anything else you can do when the population is small?

There are two possibilities:

- If the population is really small – sports centres in Derby, for example, and, to suit our purposes, let us assume there are only two – switch to a case study approach, looking at either or both. Questionnaires would be entirely inappropriate. They would, however, be appropriate if your unit of analysis (the items that make up your population) were changed to 'users of Derby sports centres'. A tweaked central research question would of course be called for.
- At the next level up, let us say that instead of investigating sports centres in Derby you decide to investigate festivals in Derby (for our purposes, let us assume there are fifteen per year). That's too many for a case study approach, but you could conduct interviews, rather than questionnaires, with senior managers of each, i.e. pick a different research method for your research design. Again, you could switch your unit of analysis – probably for each festival there are five or six organising committee members. Here you could switch from 'festivals in Derby' to 'members of their organising committees', although you would have to be careful you could keep the response rate up to a reasonable percentage.

In a nutshell:

- The size of the population has a major bearing on the most suitable research method for your project:
  - very small numbers – case study approach
  - small numbers – interviews
  - enough numbers to give you 50 completed questionnaires – questionnaires.
- You can tweak the population by opening up or closing down geographically:
  - Derby/East Midlands/England – although the last two might create serious operational problems for you!
- You can tweak the population by switching the unit of analysis.
- Very roughly the size of the chosen population leads us to different research designs and methods:
  - organisations – case studies
  - managers – interviews
  - customers/consumers – questionnaires.

Which should I go for – primary or secondary data?

Having spent some time looking at the potential snags with gathering primary data, we turn now to the pros and cons of gathering primary and secondary data. These are set out in Table 7.4 below.

TABLE 7.4   Primary v. secondary data

	Primary data	Secondary data
The pluses	You have the possibility of generating unique and innovative data.	It has already been created.
	You can aim to gather precisely the data you need.	It is generally free.
		You know from the beginning whether it is available or not.
The minuses	It can be time consuming and costly.	You are restricted to data that is already available.
	There is the added pressure of having to reach a desired sample size.	What is available may not be precisely what you want.
	There is an uncertainty hanging over whether you will able to get it.	You have no control over the quality; you are reliant on the original generator of the data.

While primary data has the key attraction of being precisely what you need, it carries with it a number of disadvantages. Providing secondary data actually consists of what you need for your research, it carries with it only one significant disadvantage – you have no control, and no guarantee over its quality. If you can establish the level of quality through a process of evaluation that it is of sufficient quality, it is often the better bet.

So how can I evaluate the quality of secondary data?

We've already noted that data from company websites is likely to be accurate, but it may tell only the positive side of the story. A better bet is secondary data from a neutral source, such as a government website.

The likelihood is that we are talking about secondary data from a web source, and thereby hangs a problem. Unlike, for example, academic journals where any data published has been subjected to a rigorous process of double-blind peer reviewing (two respected academics have reviewed the article before publication without knowing who the author of the article is), anyone can publish anything on the internet, whether or not it's true.

The first important point is to dig as deep as you can to find the original source. Wikipedia, for example, contains a lot of secondary data, but its usefulness depends on where it came from. Always click through to the sources referenced in the Wikipedia article. If there are no references cited, the data is as good as useless. Even Wikipedia itself is aware of the problem and you will often find warnings about the lack of citations in an article!

Let's assume then that you have tracked some potentially usable data down to its original internet source. How do you decide whether or not it is usable?

Robert Harris and Andrew Spinks (2007) provide a very thorough checklist at www. virtualsalt.com/evalu8it.htm.

At the heart of their evaluation system is the CARS checklist, summarised in Table 7.5 below.

TABLE 7.5   CARS checklist for evaluation of secondary data (adapted from Harris and Spinks, 2007)

Credibility	Trustworthy source, author's credentials, evidence of quality control, known or respected authority, organisational support.
	Goal: an authoritative source, a source that supplies some good evidence that allows you to trust it.
Accuracy	Up to date, factual, detailed, exact, comprehensive, audience and purpose reflect intentions of completeness and accuracy.
	Goal: a source that is correct today (not yesterday), a source that gives the whole truth.

(Continued)

TABLE 7.5   (Continued)

Reasonableness	Fair, balanced, objective, reasoned, no conflict of interest, absence of fallacies or slanted tone.
	Goal: a source that engages the subject thoughtfully and reasonably, concerned with the truth.
Support	Listed sources, contact information, available corroboration, claims supported, documentation supplied.
	Goal: a source that provides convincing evidence for the claims made, a source you can triangulate (find at least two other sources that support it).

Other useful evaluation guides are:

- The Cornell University guide
  http://olinuris.library.cornell.edu/ref/research/webeval.html
- The Purdue Online Lab
  http://owl.english.purdue.edu/owl/resource/553/01/
- The University of British Columbia guide
  http://help.library.ubc.ca/evaluating-and-citing-sources/evaluating-information-sources/

Once you have found a possible source of secondary data, use one of the guides listed above to evaluate it. Use the space below to record your evaluation.

Make a decision on whether or not to use this source. If your source fails the test, find another one and repeat the process.

If you've thought about it, you will have realised that I'm a great believer in not reinventing the wheel. But can you trust me? Of course you can! This makes an important point – you should always seek the opinions of someone who knows what they are talking about, the most obvious person being your supervisor.

Is the internet generally a reliable source?

Frankly, no it isn't – it's as simple as that! While there are loads of good reliable data available, it's all the other data which has not gone through any form of quality control that makes finding reliable and usable data like looking for a needle in a haystack. Always start from a position of being sceptical, and use the guides to convince yourself that the data you have found can be used.

Before we move on, it's worth looking briefly at the question of whether you should use the internet as a means of gathering primary data. There are, after all, a number of websites such as SurveyMonkey which allow you to put up a questionnaire so that you can get people to fill it in. Attractive though this option may seem, I would strongly advise against it in general.

The dangers are:

- You can easily lose control over who is completing your questionnaires. The 'wrong kind of person' can give you invalid data out of boredom or sheer mischief.
- By losing this control, you have lost sight of what your population (P) is. You have therefore lost sight of the sample size you need.
- You have restricted, and thus biased, your sample to a population which has access to the internet, and is geeky enough and bored enough to fill in online surveys – hardly a random sample! I for one would never fill in an online questionnaire – I have better things to do with my time.

So how can I evaluate the quality of primary data?

Let's say I end up deciding to get primary data. What do I need to consider in deciding on the data I'm going to collect?

The two main considerations are the **validity** and the **reliability** of the data.

Validity refers to whether or not the data you have gathered is actually the data you needed to gather. Supposing you wanted to find out which UK airline is the most successful financially. You might consider sending questionnaires to the executives of all UK airlines and including a direct question, 'Which UK airline is the most successful financially?' The data you got back would be valid with respect to answering the question 'Which UK airline do UK airline executives think is the most successful financially?', which is quite a significantly different question. The way to gather data with validity in order to answer the first question would be to get the official financial data available from Companies House – a small but significant difference between the two questions leads to quite different data-gathering methods. If this difference is still not clear to you, consider the situation the other way round – why isn't the financial data from Companies House valid in answering the question 'Which UK airline do UK airline executives think is the most successful financially?'

Reliability refers to how consistent your data is – would you get the same data if you repeated the data-gathering exercise? To put it another way, does your data reflect accurately

Validity

The extent to which your data actually reflects the real world you are trying to measure.

Reliability

The extent to which you would get the same data if you carried on repeating your data gathering.

the situation you are working in. For example, if you were investigating the economic impact of visiting fans on the area near a football stadium, data gathered on just one afternoon would have low reliability because it would only reflect the impact of one set of visiting fans. There would be a lot of underlying variation that you were failing to record. For example, if you were researching Plymouth Argyle, there would be a much greater impact from Exeter City fans visiting than there would be from Carlisle United fans visiting simply because there would be more Exeter fans than Carlisle fans for reasons of geography. For your data to be as reliable as possible, you would need to gather data for a number of visiting teams, ideally for every home game in the season.

Of course, you need to gather data which is reliable and valid. In Figure 7.1 the concentric circles represent the target of data you are planning to gather, and the splodges represent your actual readings.

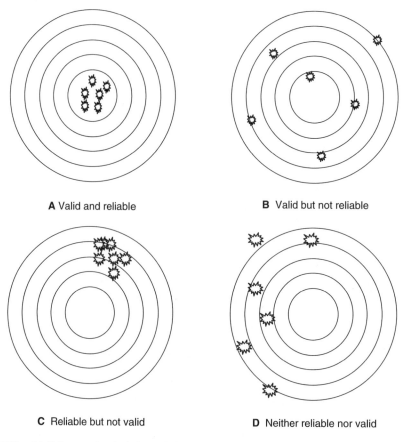

A Valid and reliable   **B** Valid but not reliable

C Reliable but not valid   **D** Neither reliable nor valid

FIGURE 7.1   Validity and reliability of data

In case A, the splodges are neatly grouped around the centre of the target, so the readings are reliable (because they are grouped closely together) and valid (they are very close to the centre of the target). In case B, they are spread out (so they are not reliable), but they are valid (because their average is near the centre of the target). In case C, the readings are reliable (because they are grouped closely together) but not valid (because their average is 'off target'). In case D, they are neither close together (and hence they are not reliable) nor is their average 'on target' (and hence they are not valid).

Let's go back to our example of researching which UK airlines are financially successful. The financial data is reliable, because Companies House would always gather exactly the same data in the same way from all the airlines.

How valid the questionnaire data would be would depend on a number of factors. We have already looked at one of them – the size of the sample. It isn't just size that matters though. We have to consider whether we have introduced a bias to our data because of the way we have gathered it.

Biases

Our (primary) data can all too easily become biased, often for reasons that we should have been able to foresee and then avoid.

 Do Reflective Exercise 3 on page 157.

The examples given there are examples of **input bias**. Bias can creep in even before we start to gather data. You will have been selective in what you have chosen to ask people about, and inevitably then your incoming data will be restricted to what you have pre-judged to be relevant. Of course you can't ask about everything, but it is good practice to be systematic in deciding what to ask. You could ask open-ended questions of interviewees during your 'pilot' phase to establish your list of topics to ask about, and you should seek the advice of your supervisor. Think in terms of having a rationale for your choice of question topics.

You need to be careful to avoid **functional fixedness** too. By this, we mean that you can be too focused on finding, for example, a 'marketing solution' to a situation because your own perspective is a marketing one. Any management lecturer will tell you that, if they give a case study to a group of marketing students, those students will offer marketing solutions. On the other hand, if they give the same case study to a group of finance students, those students will offer finance solutions. In other words,

Input bias

Bias which arises from the way you made your choice when sampling was inadvertently non-random.

Functional fixedness

Seeing a management issue from the perspective of one management function (e.g. marketing, HRM or finance) only. In other words, marketing people tend to see any management problem as a marketing problem and then look for marketing solutions.

we all tend to look for solutions to a business problem from the specialisation of our own preferred business function.

The availability, or rather, the lack of availability, of data may also introduce an input bias. If you are aware of a small and not particularly significant tranche of missing data in what you have gathered, you can simply include a mention of this (plus a justification as to why this lack of data doesn't seriously matter). If, however, the missing data is significant, you should rethink your methodology.

Probably the biggest source of input bias arises from inappropriate sampling, sampling being your choice from a population to include in your sample. As sample size is concerned with the number in your sample, so sampling is concerned with which members of the population fall within your chosen sample.

The two commonest ways of trying to avoid bias in a sample are **random sampling** and **quota sampling**.

Random sampling is precisely that – you randomly select from the population. Now random sampling sounds like a great idea, but we have just seen a major reason why it can go wrong – there are dangers of input bias in that we as humans are not very good at recognising when a selection is not actually random. If you think of the scenario used in Reflective Exercise 3, you can start to see the problem. Ignoring all the aspects of why people in the High Street on a Thursday are not themselves a random sample of the general public, we are unlikely to select people randomly to fill in our questionnaires. We may well be naturally inclined to ask attractive, friendly looking people who make eye contact rather than a truly random selection. We can reduce the bias by systematically approaching the tenth, twentieth, thirtieth, etc. person we encounter. The greater problem though lies with the potential interviewee. Some will simply decline or more aggressively refuse. Excluded from your sample will be busy people, introverted people and perhaps people who don't like students. If you think this doesn't affect randomness, consider for a moment what a world peopled entirely by these people would be like – very different from the world we actually live in, I would suggest!

Quota sampling recognises that we mere mortals don't do 'random' very well. You identify what the characteristics of the members of the population are, and you build a sample which reflects the distribution of these characteristics. For example, if 5 per cent of the population we are investigating are aged over 65, we make sure there are 5 per cent aged over 65 in our sample. It's clear that this will only work well if we actually know the characteristics of the whole population well. It can also be problematic towards the end of the sampling process. For example, we may have gathered data from 49 out of a desired sample of 50. The last person we need is a woman aged 30 to 40, married, educated to degree level, earning over £50,000 a year who lives in rented property – it may be a long wait to find this person, and the nearer we get to 'completing the set', the more difficult it becomes to find the right people.

You are never going to be able to eliminate bias completely and get the 'perfect sample' (unless of course you survey not a sample but the entire population!). What you need to

Random sampling

The process of identifying specifically who or what will constitute your sample by choosing them randomly.

Quota sampling

Choosing who or what makes up your sample so that in total they reflect the population. For example, if half the population is female, then you construct a sample which is 50 per cent female.

do is recognise any bias in your sampling and include a brief discussion in your write-up of any potential implications for the usefulness of your conclusions.

When should I be thinking of collecting data?

It is really important that you don't simply rush out and gather data, particularly if it's primary data. Until you have finalised your methodology, you don't know precisely what data you need to gather. The worst scenario is if you are using interviews as your method and the number of people whom you can interview is limited; if you've already interviewed them and then find you didn't actually ask the questions your finalised methodology dictates that you need to, well, you are in trouble.

You need to establish as early as possible a research timetable, complete with deadlines for completing each stage. Table 7.6 gives a very basic sample timetable:

TABLE 7.6   Sample timetable for doing your project

October	Drafting central research question, aims and research objectives
November	Refining central research question, aims and research objectives
December	Defining research methodology
	Choosing research methods
	Preparing research instruments
	Preparing analysis tools
January	Gathering data
February	Analysing data
March	Drawing conclusions from outputs of analysis
April	Writing up
May	Printing and binding
	Handing in

You will notice that gathering data is confined to a relatively short period in the middle of the process, which we saw previously is a reflection of the overall research design. This may have implications for what you can or cannot realistically research for your project. In Table 7.6, gathering data in January would be fine if your research design required you to interview football supporters at a football match, but would be rather bad news if you were researching cricket supporters at cricket matches or if you were investigating visitors to tourist attractions. In short, seasonality in the business market you are investigating will need to be taken into consideration. If you are from outside the UK and plan to gather data in your home country, you will need to make sure that your timetable places that data-gathering in the Christmas/New Year break.

How easy will it be to get primary data?

That obviously depends on what you are researching and how you plan to gather your primary data. My general advice is that it will be much harder to gather than you imagine. This is particularly true if you require the cooperation of the people you plan to interview or to have fill in your questionnaires. As I've said, if I had a pound for every time I've heard one of my students say, 'Well, I plan to interview the chairmen of the Premier League football clubs', well, I wouldn't be exactly rich, but I could have a good night out. The reality is of course that senior people in a sector which is notorious for secrecy and confidentiality simply will not speak to people outside their immediate environment. Many organisations have, over the years, been inundated with requests to collaborate in student projects and dissertations – the best you can hope for is a short standard reply saying 'Sorry. No'. Your best way of avoiding these issues of accessibility is to plan to exploit any personal contacts you have. This may nudge you towards researching smaller local organisations rather than big-name companies, which is no bad thing when you remember that you have to fill a gap in knowledge. The major high street chains have been researched to death by students, whereas a smaller local organisation won't have been.

A quick reminder – you will need to have complied with your university's Code of Ethics, and this will nudge you away from surveying those aged under eighteen for example.

Is secondary data going to be a better bet then?

Providing the secondary data which is available is both reliable and valid for your needs, which implies you need to have evaluated these two aspects, the answer is generally a loud 'Yes' – it's as simple as that. Remember too that, subject to the same provisions, it's far less work (and cheaper!).

OK, I've got my data – what next?

Analyse it! This should not come as a surprise as you should have prepared your analytical tools at the time of your pilot survey. The purpose of your various analyses should reflect your research objectives.

That is not to say that you should ignore any surprises that your data has thrown up. In some cases, where your literature review has shown that not much research has been done, you will be looking for the unexpected.

Bear in mind that, in designing your analysis before you gathered the data, you have prejudged what the results will be, and that judgement may be wrong. You should be looking for expected *and* unexpected patterns in the data.

Once you have come to the direct conclusions which relate to your specified research objectives, you need to relate these back to your specified aims, and ultimately back to answering the central research question. As you go through this process, you need to identify any limitations that your methodology has thrown up in answering the central research question. These may well include limitations imposed by the availability of the data, and any bias in gathering the data which you were not able to eliminate. Remember, providing these limitations are not so overwhelming as to destroy the credibility of your methodology, you will be given credit for recognising the limitations.

Chapter conclusion

By working your way through this chapter you will have moved on further from thinking about the research process in a generalised way to a much more focused view of your specific research project.

In particular you will have thought about how you will go about filling the gap in knowledge which you have identified by working through the previous chapter. You should have made progress in defining:

- A central research question
- which leads to two or three aims
- each of which leads to two or three research objectives.

You should also have given some thought to some of the more common snags which can arise when doing research, and considered how you can avoid them by tweaking your research design.

You will have thought about a number of issues relating to the data that will be used in your analysis. These issues include:

- access, availability, time costs, financial costs and seasonality
- sample structuring and issues of size
- primary v. secondary data
- the quality of data, including the concepts of reliability and validity
- the problems of bias and how they might be minimised.

1. Make sure you are familiar with the concepts listed in this summary. Go back and revisit any you are not sure about.
2. Make sure you have worked on all the 'Stop boxes', especially those which begin on page 77. Don't be afraid to revisit them later and tweak what you have written.

Recommended reading

Royer, I. and Zarlowski, P. (2001) 'Sampling' in R.-A. Thietart et al., *Doing Management Research*, London: Sage.

8

Methods

Chapter objectives

By completing the work in this chapter, you should be able to:

- develop instruments for the more common research methods:
  - prepare a questionnaire
  - design a structured interview
  - understand the case study approach

- explain the basic principles of coding.

Introduction

In this chapter we will look at the more common methods used in research projects. They are all likely to be familiar to you in the sense that you will have come across research outcomes developed using these methods.

Think of three pieces of research which you have come across using a) question-naires, b) interviews and c) the case study approach. Note these examples here:

- questionnaires
- interviews
- case study.

For each of the three, reflect on why the particular method was chosen for the particular research topic. Was it an appropriate choice of method? Why was it appropriate?

The research methods you use will be specific to your project. In looking at the different research methods we are looking at a stage in the research process which has moved on from our starting point where we could generalise about all projects. In this chapter we will therefore look at the various methods without going into great depth, and will only cover the methods which are frequently used in undergraduate projects. For your project, you should look at your chosen method in greater depth in other books which are more focused on specific methods. Recommended reading can be found in the bibliography section at the end of this book, and in 'recommended reading' boxes throughout the chapter.

A variety of research methods is available, and the choice of which to use is highly specific to the individual project. Possible choices include:

- archival sources of data
- controlled experiment with control group
- focus groups
- interviews:
  - structured (the same questions are asked at each interview)
  - unstructured (free-form interviews, where the questioning depends on the responses given by the person being interviewed)
- participant observation
- questionnaires:
  - face to face, with you asking the questions and marking down the responses
  - self-administered (usually sent electronically or through the post)
- simulation
- structured diaries/logs
- structured observation.

To this list we should add the case study. Strictly speaking this is an 'approach' rather than a 'method' in the way that the others above are methods. But it is easier to discuss as if it were a similar kind of method. In reality it is a mixed method applied in particular circumstances.

In my experience, the clear majority of student projects are built around one of three methods – questionnaires, interviews or case studies. In this chapter we will focus on these three. If you want to use one or more of the others, refer to the recommended reading.

Questionnaires and interviews involve the gathering of primary data, and are known collectively as surveys. The case study or studies may involve the gathering of both primary and secondary data although the balance between the two can be very different for different projects.

Because the choice of method is highly individual, I suggest that you:

- look at the three I have covered below
- decide which you are going to use
- look at the appropriate section again but this time be more reflective
- look at the recommended reading for the particular method (given in a box at the end of each section).

Please note that because the choice is highly individual to your project and its central research question, it may be that one of the other methods in the list above is the most appropriate – I have just expanded below on the most commonly used. Appropriateness is a key issue, and you should have a look at Reflective Exercise 5 (page 150).

Questionnaires

Questionnaires can be used to gather either (or both) quantitative and qualitative data. In order to gather qualitative data, you ask open-ended questions, where a respondent writes in their choice of response. This sounds very attractive as a way of getting the best quality of response, but it has the serious disadvantage of making analysis much more difficult. To gather quantitative data using a questionnaire, you use the most commonly used format – a questionnaire using Likert scales. The Likert scale is named after a celebrated American researcher of organisations and dates back to the 1930s.

The typical Likert scale looks like this:

TABLE 8.1   A Likert scale

Rate your response to the statement on the following scale from 1 to 5:				
Strongly agree	Agree	No preference	Disagree	Strongly disagree
1	2	3	4	5

The strength of this method is that it allows feelings and opinions from respondents to be recorded in a quantitative form which can then be processed statistically. We can use statistical methods to draw conclusions about the sample and, if the sample is big enough, we can investigate the differences between, for example, the responses of men and women within the sample.

Its weakness is that it forces respondents into only one of five possible responses. It depends on individuals interpreting the difference between, for example, 'agree' and 'strongly agree' in the same way, and assumes that responding 'strongly agree' shows the same strength of feeling in all the people who choose that response. It assumes 'strongly agree' to one statement reflects the same strength of feeling when used as a response to a different statement. In essence, it oversimplifies the measuring of responses.

A practical issue is that people tend to cluster their responses around 'no preference', or 'neither agree nor disagree' as it is often expressed. This is not terribly helpful to a researcher, and a sneaky way of avoiding this is to use a 6-point scale – the neutral response is replaced by two extra possible responses of 'slightly agree' and 'slightly disagree'. It has helped us as researchers by making sure everyone is forced to hold either a positive or a negative view, but of course is open to the criticism that it has banished all neutral responses, which is unlikely to be a realistic view of the situation.

How do I go about writing my questionnaire?

It is vital that your questionnaire gathers the specific data that you will need for your analysis. It must have a purpose, which is, by definition, to help you answer your central research question. If you cast your mind back to the three levels in the research design hierarchy, you will remember that in your design you have moved down the hierarchy to the level of research objectives, which are relatively specific, and, I argued, give a hint as to how they will be achieved.

Each of your research objectives becomes, in effect, a heading within your questionnaire, although I am definitely not suggesting that you should actually write each of these 'headings' into your questionnaire – you need to know they are there, but your respondents don't!

For each research objective, you need to write a specific set of questions which will allow you to achieve that objective. There is no magic answer to the question 'How many questions for each research objective?' The answer will depend on how focused the research objective is, and whether it is 'multi-layered', in other words, how many elements there are within the individual research objective.

It follows that you may well have different numbers of questions for each research objective. This is quite natural, and nothing to worry about. What you do need to worry about is the total number of questions, as this will have a major bearing on how long the questionnaire will take to complete. When you have piloted and refined your questionnaire, you will have a good idea of how long that is. Ask yourself whether this is a reasonable amount of time to engage with a single respondent. Again, there is no magic length of time. It will depend on how interested your respondents are in the topic. If you were interviewing fans of a football club, they would be much more willing to spend time talking about what merchandising they have bought or will buy, for example, rather than about their thoughts on the debt level and projected cashflow of their club.

Next comes a vital but rather tricky stage – you need to evaluate how well the questions will work in practice. The kinds of things you need to think about (particularly in the light of your experience from piloting the material) are:

- Will my respondents actually be able to respond? Have I assumed, perhaps wrongly, that they have the knowledge and/or experience to respond meaningfully?
- Will respondents understand the statements or questions in the way that I mean them? Is there any danger that they are in some way ambiguous? Have I used language that is appropriate? If you are working on a topic that has its own jargon, the creative industries for example, there is no problem in using that jargon if your respondents are by definition practitioners within that industry. However, using jargon would be silly if you were trying to assess the potential of marketing to the general public by asking members of the general public for their responses. For similar reasons, be wary of using 'yoofspeak'[1] if you are going to be interviewing people of all ages.
- Is everything I plan to include in the questionnaire spelt correctly (use Spellcheck – the clue is in the name), grammatically correct and free from typing errors generally? Is the layout on the pages attractive? Getting any of these wrong will simply encourage some respondents to abandon filling in your questionnaire.

Next you need to think about the order and the form of the statements or questions. Tips here are:

- Avoid the 'double negative trap'. By this I mean don't write statements or questions that require the respondent to use mental gymnastics to work out whether they agree or disagree. An example of bad practice would be: '(How strongly do you agree or disagree that) the absence of a logo on individual pieces of chocolate doesn't affect your enjoyment of the chocolate?' The use of 'doesn't' is obviously one of the negative elements in what you are asking, but the use of 'absence' is a much less obvious negative (absence means something not being present when you would expect it to be present). A better way to formulate this question would be: '(How strongly do you agree or disagree that) the presence of a logo on individual pieces of chocolate affects the enjoyment of the chocolate?'
- Make sure that respondents don't tend too much towards one end of the Likert scales when they respond to individual statements or answer individual questions. For example, let's imagine you ask for responses to the two statements: 'Virgin offers products which are good value for money' and 'Virgin's products are high-quality products at affordable prices.' The same person is likely to respond in very similar ways. It would be better to rephrase the first statement as: 'Virgin offers products which are poor value for money' – the same person would then have to respond at different ends of the spectrum. This not only 'keeps the respondent on their toes' but ensures that they use the whole range of values over the whole questionnaire – it avoids them almost mindlessly prejudging their response and just using either the left end or the right end of the response scales.

---

[1] By 'yoofspeak' I mean the casual and relaxed language you use when only with your fellow students – the kind of language that might puzzle your parents and totally confuse your gran.

Once you have the first complete draft of your statements/questions, go back to our earlier review of bias and check that you haven't fallen into one of the bias traps. And think very carefully about any possible bias because you have not asked about some important issue! Redraft your questions as necessary.

Now is the time to decide exactly:

- Who you are going to ask?

- How you are going to get them to do your questionnaire?

- When and where are you going to get them to complete your questionnaire?

It is always a good idea to develop a Plan B for the above box – what is your fall-back position if your response rate proves too low? In other words, if you don't get enough completed questionnaires through Plan A, what are you going to do to retrieve the situation?

The essential process of piloting your questionnaire allows you to identify any potential shortcomings in the way you have written your questionnaire. Remember to make sure that the pilot is used with people who represent the sample you will actually be using. Just piloting it with your mates when you plan to survey the general public will not pick up any problems through using 'yoofspeak', for example.

If questionnaires are your chosen method, dig deeper into the subject by looking at the recommended reading in the box below.

Recommended reading

Bourqe, L. and Fielder E.P (2002) *How to Conduct Self-Administered and Mail Surveys* (2nd edn), London: Sage.

Fink, A. (2008) *How to Conduct Surveys* (4th edn), Newbury Park: Sage.

Foddy, W. (1994) *Constructing Questions for Interviews and Questionnaires*, Cambridge: Cambridge University Press.

Oppenheim, A.N. (2000) *Questionnaire Design, Interviewing and Attitude Measurement*, London: Continuum.

Ornstein, M. (2013) *A Companion to Survey Research*, London: Sage.

Interviews

Before committing yourself to using the interview method, be absolutely sure that you will get access to the people you need to interview! Remember that you may have left yourself with no way back to completing your project in time if you suddenly find that, late on in the process, doors to vital offices fail to open.

There are two main variants to the interview. The first is the structured interview, where you ask every interviewee exactly the same set of specific questions, working from your 'cribsheet', which is not a million miles different from a sophisticated questionnaire. Unlike the questionnaire, where you are forcing responses into a number on a Likert scale, you encourage the interviewee to elaborate their thoughts – the question is a prompt to get them talking in a structured way. You can refer to the section above on questionnaires for thoughts on how to compose the questions you are going to ask. The only difference is that you are invariably composing questions rather than statements to express an opinion on, and you have much more freedom, in that you can ask 'How?' and 'Why?' The structure you impose relates in the same way to your research objectives as the questionnaire statements and provides a framework for your analysis.

In the same way as with a questionnaire you need to have some idea beforehand of how long the interview is going to last, but you will find it much more difficult to estimate. In an ideal world you would be able to pilot the interview, but as you are likely to be interviewing people in senior positions in organisations, it may be difficult to find 'guinea pigs'. You may have to rapidly decide to cut down the list of questions in the light of your early experience, but be careful to make sure your cutting down doesn't result in you failing to cover questions on one of your research objectives.

You will need to think ahead in terms of how long you ask someone to make themselves available for interview – they can't 'do it in their own time' like a self-administered questionnaire, and probably you will need to interview them in their workplace during the working day.

Interviewees may be reluctant to talk in case they find what they say being reported in some public place to their possible embarrassment. This can usually be avoided by explaining when setting up the interview that you will conduct the interview under what is known as the 'Chatham House Rule'. This rule is widely used among politicians and journalists to allow information to be given by the former to the latter without any fear of comeback. You will have inadvertently come across its use every time you read in a newspaper 'a senior official said' or 'a source close to the Cabinet Office said'. The formal definition of the rule is:

When a meeting, or part thereof, is held under the *Chatham House Rule*, participants are free to use the information received, but neither the identity nor the affiliation of the speaker(s), nor that of any other participant, may be revealed. (Chatham House, 2014)

To give you an example of how this works in practice, during my PhD research I interviewed thirty members of the boards of UK airlines. To give my thesis some credibility, I actually listed them in alphabetical order in an appendix. I gave each of them a code in the series [I01], [I02], [I03], etc. (the 'I' stands for interviewee), with the numbers reflecting the order in which I interviewed them, which only I knew. Providing I was careful with the words I chose to describe individual interviewees, it did not prove difficult to quote their words in the thesis, as appropriate, without revealing their identity.

It is good practice to record your interviews and produce a transcript of each interview – it's much more effective than relying on your note-taking skills. Once you have explained that you will be abiding by the Chatham House Rule, you will find much less objection to your recording the interview. Of the thirty people interviewed for my thesis, twenty-nine had no objection to my recording the interview, and the other one simply asked me to delete the recording and transcript when I had finished using them – not a problem.

As we noted earlier, the data from interviews is much richer than that from questionnaires, which does, however, make analysis more complicated. The usual way of doing this is to 'code' the transcript. You work your way through the transcripts marking up key themes or ideas expressed. Each theme or code is a label so that you can identify where different interviewees have expressed similar ideas. What the codes are will in part be something you can predict, but they should include new ideas (new to you, that is) that emerge from the interviews. Once you have coded the full set of transcripts you can use the coding as a basis for analysis, identifying who said what in conceptual terms, how frequently it was said, and whether pairs of ideas were expressed together.

You shouldn't simply do the coding yourself – remember the ever-present issue of bias. Enlist a couple of fellow students to code the transcripts too – this will prove easier than you might think if you return the favour by coding their transcripts for them as well. Any disagreements on the actual coding should be negotiated to agreement.

Your university may have software available to make coding and analysis easier for you. The most common package is called NVivo. Learning to use the software may well take you some time, so you would need to allow for this in your research timetable – early in the timetable of course!

Recommended reading

Kvale, S. (2008) *Doing Interviews*, London: Sage.

Rubin, H.J. and Rubin, I.S. (2012) *Qualitative Interviewing*, London: Sage.

Case studies

Generally you choose a case study approach for reasons different from those for using other approaches. The driving force is perhaps not the desire to answer a central research question which sprang up in your mind, but rather more the curiosity you have for the particular organisation or organisations that will form the case(s). This immediately highlights the possible danger of doing a case study – you may end up describing an organisation, albeit with some new insight, without making any significant contribution to the body of knowledge. Be clear then that even with a case study you need to have a precise central research question. The chances are that the question will begin with either 'How?' or 'Why?' – it is likely that you will be unravelling complex issues. The case study approach is definitely not an easy option.

Although you are largely driven by curiosity, it may well be that underlying your curiosity is a familiarity with the organisation – familiar enough to engage with it and perhaps even have great access opportunities. This serves as a warning that you may in fact be too close to the organisation and may already have preconceived ideas of what the answer to your central research question is – beware of your personal prejudices, or, in another word, bias.

Now don't get me wrong. I'm not trying to put you off doing a case study. I'm simply saying that, while it may seem attractive because of your natural interest in the organisation, it has its own difficulties.

Think carefully about how someone else might see your choice of organisation. Will they just think it's you indulging in your obsession, or will they see your research as worthwhile and interesting?

Now, so far I've assumed you have chosen one organisation, or, to put it another way, a single case study. It is possible to adopt a double or even multiple case study approach. For an undergraduate project, I would generally advise sticking to a single case study simply on the grounds of the size of the research project – you won't have the time to investigate more than one organisation deeply enough.

So, where did the inspiration for your choice of case come from? As often as not, it will be an opportunistic decision. You will have chosen an organisation which is familiar to you, which is local, maybe even one you have worked for, or one where you happen to have really good contacts and thus a good chance of access. There's nothing wrong with that, but you will need, in writing up your project, to justify your choice, and none of the reasons I've just given count as a justification. You will need to make a case that your chosen case is either one of the following:

- an exceptional case, far from the typical case, and therefore worthy of investigation
- an absolutely typical case, and hence one from which you will be able to generalise your conclusions to other cases.

Remember, it's not just a question of convincing yourself that, say, your local branch of a DIY chain or local grassroots football club is either exceptional or absolutely typical – half way in between is a complete waste of time – it's a question of convincing the people who will be marking your project, that is, your supervisor and another lecturer in your university department. Your supervisor is therefore someone you need to convince at an early stage in the project process.

Triangulation

In pursuing a case study approach, you will have to dig deeply into your chosen organisation in your search for the ultimate explanation of why it functions the way it does. This means getting many different sets of data, using a variety of methods. In your analysis, you will aim to establish the same conclusions from at least two sets of data. This is known as triangulation, a term borrowed from navigation. You take bearings of an object from two different known fixed points and this allows you to calculate the precise location of the object. Similarly, two pieces of analysis allow you to confirm a tentative conclusion drawn from a previous piece of analysis.

Avoiding the essentially descriptive

Even if you manage to avoid the trap of choosing a case to study which is in some way your favourite choice rather than one that is demonstrably exceptional or demonstrably typical, there is a second trap awaiting you – there is a distinct danger that you will end up simply describing the complexities within the case organisation you have chosen to investigate. As with all research, you will need to produce a rigorous analysis and synthesis of the organisation. You don't want to find the marker of the project thinking, 'And your point is?' or 'So what?' Even with a case study you need to follow the familiar pattern which starts with a central research question asked about your chosen organisation.

 Recommended reading

Remenyi, D. (2012) *Case Study Research (The Quick Guide)*, Sonning Common: Academic Publishing International.

Yin, R.K. (2008) *Case Study Research: Design and Methods* (4th edn), London: Sage.

Other approaches

There are of course many other general research designs which you can adopt for your project; we have only looked at those which are more commonly chosen. My advice is to follow one of these well-worn paths – past students have chosen them for good reasons.

This is not to say that you cannot use one of the other approaches, but to do so is taking a bit of a risk, and you would need to read up that approach in another book.

Chapter conclusion

In this chapter we have looked at various research methods which can be used in gathering the data you will need for research.

In particular we have looked at the three most often used in ungraduated projects:

- questionnaires
- interviews
- case studies.

The choice of method will depend on your choice of topic. In other words, you will need to choose a research method which is appropriate. Although you will need to feel comfortable with your choice, your personal comfort must not be the deciding factor – appropriateness, not comfort, is the key!

We've reached the point where you will be starting down a very specific research path – your content. It's therefore important to focus on your needs rather than review all the methods which we have looked at.

To round off the chapter go back and work on choosing the research method which is appropriate to your project by completing the box below.

 Which basic research method is the appropriate one for answering your central research question? Why? Are there any alternatives?

Section conclusion

In this section, which comprises Chapters 6, 7 and 8, we have started to focus very specifically on your project. You should have developed, by completing the various write-in boxes and reflection boxes, clear ideas on your:

- literature search and thence literature review
- methodology, reflecting on how your chosen perspective – phenomenological or positivist – will influence your research design
- appropriate research methods for your project.

If you have been using the book properly, this will not just exist in your head, but will have been set down by you in this book.

SECTION 4

Analysing your results and writing up

Section guide

In this section, which comprises Chapters 9 and 10, we will focus on the analysis and synthesis of the data you will have gathered, and how you can use this to tick off your research objectives, and hence your aims, and thus achieve a suitable answer to your central research question.

We will be looking at how to:

- analyse the results of your data-gathering, and from your analysis synthesise your conclusions (Chapter 9)
- write up your project for handing in (Chapter 10).

This will involve looking at the writing-up process, the part of the whole schema which is most obviously and literally 'producing a project' if we see the project simply as the outcome of the whole process, in other words, what you physically hand in.

9

Analysis and Synthesis

Chapter objectives

By completing the work in this chapter, you should be able to:

- plan the analysis and synthesis of your data
- appreciate the restricted usefulness of analytical tools as opposed to the considerably greater usefulness of theoretical frameworks.

Introduction

In this chapter we will look at some general themes of analysing and synthesising data. In doing so, you will have the opportunity to develop an analytical framework for your own project.

What do I do once I've gathered all my data?

Oh dear! This is the 'wrong' question.

If you had been following the thread of the book, you would have planned this at an earlier stage, and would even have had a dummy run at analysing your data once you had gathered some data at the pilot stage.

Not to worry – we will look at some general principles of analysis and synthesis, but if you have already gathered all your data without going through a pilot stage and a dummy run, you need to be aware of a couple of possible problems: you may not have gathered exactly the data you actually need, or you may have gathered data that will be difficult to analyse. In the worst-case scenario, you may not be able to reach the research objectives you set yourself.

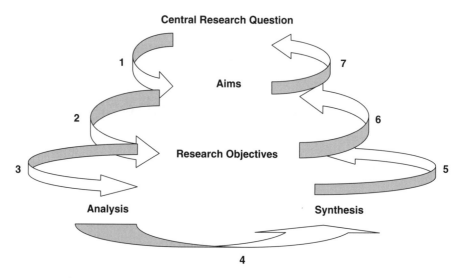

FIGURE 9.1   The seven steps to achieving an awesome logic

What you are aiming for in your analysis and synthesis is to reverse the awesome logic you aimed for in your research design and take your argument all the way back to your central research question (see Figure 9.1). You will have reached a critical point when you come to analyse your data and synthesise the results. The key question is whether you really can draw all this back to answering your central research question.

If you can, result! If you can't, it will be either because of a weakness in your design, or a slip-up in gathering your data. Recovering from this 'fail' is tricky, and success isn't guaranteed. Your only likely possibility is to see if you can tweak your central research question, aims and/or research objectives to fit with the data you've gathered and the analysis and synthesis possible from this data. A less likely possibility is that you might be able to gather your data set again, but this time making sure it is the right set of data for your chosen design.

Getting the most out of your data

In an ideal world you will have pre-planned what exactly it is that you want to get out of your data in terms of analysis and synthesis. You will have 'pre-guessed' or anticipated the kind of patterns that will emerge.

Surprise, surprise, we don't live in an ideal world! Firstly, you may have anticipated wrongly. Sure, you may know your topic well, but remember that we are looking for a gap in knowledge, something that we don't actually know for certain yet. It would be a funny old world if we always guessed correctly what the things we don't know actually turn out to be. There would be no surprises, and surprise outcomes of research are not only perfectly acceptable but actually far more interesting. Who knows, you may even have stumbled across something which will lead to further research! If they are surprise results, you will need to think about why they are surprising. Go back and ask yourself questions like:

- Was my data biased in some way that I hadn't anticipated?
- Was my sample big enough?
- Was my sample badly constructed?

If your answers are deeply worrying, you have a problem. In your write-up, you will have to 'fess up' in a section called 'limitations'. You may feel tempted to try and ignore the problem, but acknowledging such a problem in your write-up (your finished project, in other words) will gain you more credit than letting your supervisor work out the existence of the problem for him/herself when marking.

Secondly, you may have come across something which nobody might have anticipated. Typically this means finding a high level of correlation between two sets of data. For example, this might be that men and women correlate at different levels with some variable you have measured. The most likely reason for this is that your sample size was small, and you just happened to pick particular men and women who produced the surprising result – beware of what are known as 'spurious correlations', apparent correlations that have only shown up because of the fact that you have looked at a limited number of examples which do not in fact reflect the results you would have got if you had looked at the whole population. Spurious correlations are liable to come up if you indulge yourself in what is known as data mining – conducting every possible statistical analysis of the data you have. Just stick to the analyses and tests that are appropriate.

It's worth considering if there might be some underlying reason for any difference between two groups in your sample. For 'men' v. 'women' this may be unfruitful, but if the difference is between 'young people' and 'old people' you might be able to think of explanations related to their different upbringings, their different attitudes or their different experiences. Be a little cautious in placing too much value on these differences – they represent only part of your sample, i.e. the value of n is lower, and so you can only have a lower level of confidence in your conclusions. Again, your musings should nevertheless be included in your write-up.

Statistical tests

There are many, many statistical tests that are used in the analysis of quantitative data. You need to gather the data which is appropriate for your chosen test, so you need to think about which test you are going to use before you gather data!

Statistics and statistical tests are beyond the scope of this book. I will assume that you fall into one of two categories of students:

- the student who has chosen a positivist perspective, and who will be using statistical tests during the analysis of his/her data, but who did not break into a sweat when the statistics lectures were delivered
- the student who has chosen a phenomenological perspective, and who did break into a sweat when the statistics lectures were being delivered, but who will not be using statistical tests during the analysis of his/her data.

Neither of these two types of students particularly needs the basic guidance that would be in a book written at this level on the general subject of doing a research project.

For the few students who fall between these two categories, I will confine myself to steering you towards some recommended reading. The books I recommend are aimed at students who want a very low-level entry into statistics.

 Recommended reading

If you need to brush up on your statistics, either go for an old favourite (which may or may not include your lecture notes from earlier modules which were designed to prepare you for the project) or look at one of the many excellent new books that are being published. You can do a lot worse than:

Diamantopoulos, A. and Schlegelmilch, B.B. (1997) *Taking the Fear out of Data Analysis*, London: Thompson Learning.

This actually helps with the problem of choosing the appropriate statistical technique, or you might try:

Salkind, Neil J. (2010) *Statistics for People Who (Think They) Hate Statistics* (4th edn), Thousand Oaks: Sage.

Be aware of one classic difficulty with correlations. Correlations are not proof of a causal connection. For example, you may have found a correlation between variable A and variable B. It does not follow that A causes B. It may be that B causes A, or that both A and B are actually caused by a third variable C. So don't make unfounded claims that you have shown that A causes B. At best, you have found 'indicative evidence' rather than 'proof'. Figure 9.2 shows diagrammatically three different forms of causality which will all show correlation between A and B.

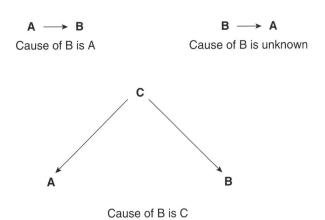

Cause of B is C

Three different causes of B, but in each case there will be correlation between A and B

FIGURE 9.2   Three different causalities which show the same correlation

Remember I suggested you need to get as much analysis out of your data as possible? At the very least go back and check that you have actually used all the data you have gathered. After all, what is the point in gathering it in the first place if you are not going to use it? After your pilot stage and your initial run at analysis, you should have identified redundant data, and decided either not to gather it in your main data-gathering work, or decided what use you were going to put it to.

In general …

By now we have reached the point where every project has become so individual that it is not possible to offer you some generalised template of how to conduct analysis. What can be said is that you are looking for patterns, whether your data is qualitative or quantitative.

If qualitative, you will be going over text, attempting to find patterns through the use of coding (see page 106).

If quantitative, you need to consider the various ways you can use statistical tests. The series of questions you need to answer revolves around deciding which test, or rather tests, you should use. As there is no general answer to this question, you need to go through a systematic process of deciding what data sets you have and which tests are appropriate for exploring relationships between them. The process is beyond the scope of this book, but if you have chosen a research design that involves statistical analysis you may well want some basic support:

- I would recommend as a starting point the excellent webpage at http://depts.alverno. edu/nsmt/stats.htm. It starts at the most basic of levels, unlike most other online guides, and talks you through in a clear step-by-step way.
- Once you have mastered that, try this webpage: http://people.umass.edu/evagold/ excel.html. It's more complicated, but it takes that necessary step deeper into the process.
- A very useful decision tree for deciding which test is appropriate can be found at www. microsiris.com/Statistical%20Decision%20Tree/ together with a very useful glossary of terms at www.microsiris.com/Statistical%20Decision%20Tree/Glossary.htm.

 If your attempts at engaging with statistical tests don't seem to be turning out well, check out the maths support that your university offers.

Remembering your literature review

Theoretical framework

An evidence-based framework, tried and tested by an academic, which can be applied in other circumstances.

Analytical tool

A device which can be used to help you analyse a situation. Unlike a theoretical framework, it may lack rigorous testing based on evidence.

In Chapter 6 we saw that one of the functions of conducting a literature review is to identify the already established theories that are relevant to your research. You have thus established a set of tools which you not only can use, but indeed should use, for your analysis and synthesis.

We need to distinguish two kinds of tools you can use – theoretical frameworks and analytical tools. It is vital that you understand the difference between them.

Theoretical frameworks, or just plain theories, have the following characteristics:

- They have been proposed and tested by academics. The testing involves gathering research data. They are thus evidence based.
- The results of these tests, and hence the confirmation that the theory is sound, have been published in academic journals, and possibly reported subsequently in textbooks with citations of the original journal articles.
- They have the power of prediction – it is these predictions that are tested.

In the scientific world, a proven theory becomes known generally as a law, but in the less precise world of management theories continue to be called theories even when proven.

Analytical tools, on the other hand, are often simply 'rules of thumb' for ordering complex information in a way that allows us to make more sense of it. Examples from the world of management are SWOT analysis, PEST analysis and the 4Ps of marketing. They lack the power of theories to make predictions that can be verified by testing. They therefore lack the potential as research tools to make a contribution to the body of knowledge or fill a gap in the research literature.

By definition, analytical tools dodge the whole question of synthesis.

This is not to say that analytical tools are useless. They are extremely useful in the real world of business, and managers frequently use them to reduce complex information to something comprehensible. But, for the project you are undertaking, they lack academic rigour – they are not appropriate to building the logical case you need to build to establish your contribution to the body of knowledge. You may use them, but on their own, without the use of theoretical frameworks, they are insufficient.

For a successful project, you need to use theoretical frameworks as the basis for analysing your research data. They lead to testable predictions – analytical tools just lead to neat piles of sorted data!

Sources of theoretical frameworks for your project

Start by looking in the textbooks for the modules which are appropriate for your choice of topic. But beware of picking analytical tools rather than theoretical frameworks. You are more likely to fall into this trap if you use books written by and/or for practitioners – people who work in management – as opposed to textbooks written by academics for students.

You may well find that textbooks are not specific enough to your particular topic. The richest source of appropriate theoretical frameworks is academic journals. In recent years life has been made easy for you. In the bad old days you had to sit in the library and plough through endless academic journals. Today you can search academic journals by using specialist databases. These are available to you from your university's e-library. If you are unsure about how to access this, ask at your library's Help Desk.

Academics nowadays often publish their articles on the internet as well as in academic journals, and these you can find by using search engines such as Google. But herein lies a serious problem: Google will pull up anything that has been published on the net – there is absolutely no guarantee of any quality control on what has been put on a website. For example, at one time, just to make this point, I had a webpage on Coventry University's server that set out 'Beech's Law of Porcine Aviation', which stated that pigs can indeed fly.

On the other hand, academic journal articles have been quality controlled by:

- two or three other academics who have blind-reviewed (i.e. not knowing who the author is) the article before publication
- the editor of the journal, who is usually a leading academic.

Fortunately for you, Google recognised that there was an issue here, and has thoughtfully established Google Scholar (http://scholar.google.com/), which conveniently only searches through academic articles available on the net.

Chapter conclusion

This chapter has taken you through some of the issues which arise in deciding how to analyse and synthesise data. These need to be applied to your specific research project, so, before moving on to the next chapter, make sure you spend some time completing the 'Stop box' below.

Which theoretical frameworks will provide you with insight in your project? You can use the write-in box on page 109 as a starting point.

Is there a good match between what you wrote back then and what you are thinking now? If there are significant differences, you have drifted in your research process, and you may have to go back and tweak your central research question, your aims and your objectives to keep the thread of your research aligned.

Recommended reading

Fink, A. (2003) *How to Manage, Analyze and Interpret Survey Data* (2nd edn), Thousand Oaks: Sage.

Remenyi, D., Onofrei, G. and English, J. (2009) *An Introduction to Statistics Using Microsoft Excel*, Reading: Academic Publishing International.

10

Writing Up

Chapter objectives

By completing the work in this chapter, you should be able to:

- define the structure of the project for handing in as required at your university
- understand the rationale of that structure
- appreciate the style of writing
- participate in any online plagiarism testing required by your university.

Introduction

We've now reached what might seem to be the final phase of 'producing your project', but it will become clear that some writing-up can take place early on in the whole project-writing process.

It is really important that you use an appropriate writing style – one that is more formal than the one I have been using, and yet one which does not sound pompous when read out loud.

Using online plagiarism detection software, the most common example being Turnitin, is becoming standard practice at universities, and so we will be looking at the implications of this.

How do I set about writing it up?

There are three aspects to writing up that you need to consider:

1. The physical production of your project in the right format.
2. The technical specification, laid down by your university, on issues like font, font size and spacing.
3. The practical question of what to write in each chapter.

 Find and print off the requirements of your university for issues 1 and 2 above, and for issue 3 if they lay down what to write where.
You should have already printed off your university's technical specification (see page 37).

I am going to offer no advice on issues 1 and 2 as I assume you will have to do these processes in a way which will be laid down by your university, and any suggestions from me will only cause confusion.

For issue 3 above, I will offer advice. Even if your university has laid down precisely what to write and where to place it in each chapter, the following should prove useful as it offers a rationale for writing up in the specific way demanded of you.

We'll start with a basic list of chapter headings in Table 10.1.

TABLE 10.1   Outline of a project's structure chapter by chapter

- *Title page*
- *Signed declaration of originality and copyright acknowledgement*
- *Abstract*
- *Acknowledgements (if any)*
- *List of contents*
- *List of tables and figures*
- Introduction
- Literature review
- Statement of central research question; aims and objectives
- Methodology and methods
- Main corpus (description of research results and their analysis)
  (This may well consist of a number of chapters)
- Conclusions (synthesis)
- Proposals and limitations where appropriate
- *Bibliography*
- *Appendices where applicable*
  NB Italicised items do not normally count towards the word count

Let's now look at each of the chapters in a little more detail (see Table 10.2):

TABLE 10.2   Detail of a project's structure chapter by chapter

Title page	This repeats the title which appears on the cover, using any template prescribed by your university.
	Your title should not be a restatement of the central research question, but a pithy title defining the subject matter. It may include phrases like 'An Investigation into', 'An Examination of', or it may specify the topic. Think carefully about the need to state limits, e.g. 'in the West Midlands'.
Signed declaration	You must sign and date the 'Declaration of originality and copyright acknowledgement' or similar form prescribed by your university.
Abstract	The abstract must be an accurate summary of the research and its findings. It can only be written after everything else has been written, and should be written in the present tense.
Acknowledgements (if any)	These should be confined to a) academic advisers and b) industry professionals who provided help. It is not appropriate to thank friends and family for general support – you should do this verbally, not in the submitted project. If you really want to include acknowledgements to parents and/or partners, do this in an extra print-off of your project, but not in the copy you hand in.
List of contents	This lists all the chapter titles, with the corresponding page numbers.
	You should not subdivide the list except if you have more than one chapter in a particular section.
List of tables and figures	Not the actual tables and figures, just a list of them. Again, you should give the corresponding page numbers.
Introduction	This simply sets the scene – the broad context in terms of business function and industry sector. It may describe briefly any appropriate historical context. It will also clarify your personal position (if any), although this should not be written in an anecdotal personal way.
Literature review	This identifies:
	a) any literature which covers both the business function and the industry sector – this will lead to identifying the gap in knowledge where you plan to make a contribution
	b) any literature on the business function which you will use for analysis and synthesis; also any apparently appropriate literature which you have actively chosen to reject, with the reasons why you have rejected it, e.g. it is not appropriate for your specific project, together with an explanation, such as rejecting US material that would not be appropriate in a UK context for reasons of business culture or organisation
	c) as for b) but with respect to the industry sector.
	The dual functions of the literature review are i) defining your potential contribution and ii) setting out the theoretical frameworks you will be using.

(Continued)

TABLE 10.2   (Continued)

Statement of central research question	The central research question must be a) a question, not just a topic for research and b) a research question as opposed to a question for journalism. In essence, the answer to your central research question will be your contribution to the body of knowledge.
Aims and research objectives	The aims break the question into more specific parts, which in turn generate the objectives of your research. In other words, you answer the question by achieving the objectives. If you end up with six objectives, each of the six must be addressed in the work that follows.
Methodology and methods	The methodology explains how you are going to answer the question – what perspective, what approach – and why this is the best way of answering it.
	The methods are the practical tools you choose as a result of your preferred methodology.
Description of research, the results and their analysis	Here you describe the actual research you undertook, report the results and analyse them using the key theoretical frameworks you flagged up in your literature review.
	This normally consists of a number of chapters, the chapters being derived from your aims and objectives.
Conclusions (synthesis)	Here you draw together the research outcomes and synthesise them from the stated research objectives, through the aims, and back to the central research question.
Proposals, and limitations, where appropriate	Proposals may relate to a) further research and/or b) suggestions to the people involved in the industry sector, with specific reference to the organisations you investigated.
	Limitations will include any limitations on how much your findings can be generalised to other situations, and practical limitations that constrained you in carrying out the data-gathering.
References	This is the list of articles, books, websites, etc. you have cited in the rest of the project. It should not include books etc. which have been consulted but not cited. It must use the Harvard convention. All entries should be in one list, ordered alphabetically by author – do not have a separate list for websites, for example. Do not use footnotes or chapter-by-chapter references.
Appendices where applicable	These contain data only included for reference. They would typically include a sample completed questionnaire, an interview proforma, etc.

It's only when you come to write up that you actually face the problem of dividing up the word limit between the chapters.

The actual word limit varies from university to university (so check what yours is!) – it's generally around 10,000 words, but may be different for project modules which carry fewer CATS points as part of your degree. Most universities (but not necessarily yours, so, again, check!) will not include items like the Table of Contents or any Appendices in the overall word count. You will then generally be left with the following chapters which do count towards the word limit:

- introduction
- literature review
- statement of central research question, aims and research objectives
- methodology and methods
- description of research, the results and their analysis and synthesis
- conclusions, proposals and limitations.

There is no perfect way of dividing the total number across these chapters; after all, it will vary from project to project. For example, I once had a student whose project was about book rental in Malaysia; clearly her literature review was by definition very short – there was very little previous research that was even indirectly relevant.

You should begin by dividing the 10,000 words (or however many it is at your university) across the six chapters listed above on a rough basis. This is not likely to be an equal number for each. 'Description of research, the results and their analysis and synthesis' is likely to be longer than 'Introduction' for example. As you adjust the number allocated to each chapter, always bear in mind that the total number must remain the same, so adding say 500 words to the allocation for one chapter must be accompanied by the deduction of 500 words somewhere else.

When should I write up?

With the exception of the Introduction, I would strongly recommend that you at least draft each chapter, chapter by chapter, as you proceed through the process. There is of course the temptation to put off writing up until the hand-in deadline is approaching. Not only is this a highly risky approach in that you may end up having to write an awful lot in a very short period of time, but also you would be writing up work which you had done several months previously, and it would no longer be fresh in your mind. With good time management, you should be able to revisit each chapter when you have completed the full drafting of the project. This is essential really as you may well find that the design and carrying out of the research process have shown some 'drift' from your original intentions.

Write the Introduction once you have written all the other chapters – it is here that you would otherwise find the greatest drift, and hence the greatest need for a rewrite. As the very last piece of writing, write the Abstract, again to avoid drift and rewriting.

This allows you to set yourself a target length for each chapter, and you should try to keep to that target. If you go over-target, you will face an agonising decision: having to cut out and scrap the surplus you have written in order to keep to the overall word count. The alternative is that you can stay over-target, and lower the target for the as yet unwritten chapters, which simply gives you the same problem with later chapters. The simple guideline is: never write too much – to do so gives you painful decisions, that is, the pain of choosing which words, words that you have already spent precious time so carefully crafting, to scrap. Ouch! By monitoring your actual word count as you proceed chapter by chapter, you will have a good idea of how much more work you have to do.

What sort of style of writing should I use?

I can't emphasise too strongly not the style I have written this book in! Remember that I deliberately chose an almost spoken style of English to make it easier to follow. Written English style, especially in academic books, can be a bit pompous and hard going for the reader as a result, which does not help in getting ideas over to the reader.

When I talked of how I had tried to write this book in a style of English that was nearer to the style of spoken English than the style of written English which you are more used to reading, I pointed out that even with spoken English there is a range of styles, and how you actually use different styles varies, for example, when talking to your mates or to your grandparents.

There is one really important message on styles that you need to take on board – don't use this informal style I am using when writing up your project. This may seem strange, but let me point out that when you studied Shakespeare back in your school-days, any textbooks commenting on his great plays and sonnets were not written in the rhyming couplets that Shakespeare himself produced. In a similar way, I've written in a way to make ideas accessible, but when you write your project you use a more formal and different style.

 Some thoughts on styles of English

The style you should aim for is a natural form of Plain English. Avoid being pompous and long-winded – it's not a written version of the proverbial policeman giving evidence in court saying, 'I was proceeding at a steady pace in a westerly direction' when he means 'I was walking west'! Compare the two versions – what the second has and the first doesn't are two vital characteristics: conciseness and clarity.

Two particular features are often associated with written English, and I will offer guidelines rather than rules:

- *The first person*

  By 'first person' we mean the words 'I' and 'me', or 'we' and 'us'. There are different views on their use in projects, so sound out your supervisor on their preference. Generally there has been a feeling that it should not be used for projects, as research is supposed to be objective and impersonal, but some more radical supervisors may encourage its use.

- *The passive voice*

  By 'passive voice' I'm referring to the form of the verb in the expression 'observations were made [by me]', as opposed to the opposite, the active voice, which would in this example be 'I made observations'. As with the question of using the first person, you can see that the issue is about how objective and impersonal the result is. Traditionalists favour the use of the passive, but more modernist supervisors may encourage the use of the active voice (in other words, using 'I').

As I said, both issues are a matter of preference and convention, importantly for you the preference and convention of those who will be marking, so check with your supervisor – most universities will specify that your supervisor can be asked to read one complete chapter of your project at some stage during the year, and this provides an excellent opportunity to get the appropriate feedback on your style.

If you are worried about your style, or feel that 'written English' is not the sharpest tool in your skills toolbox, check out the general support which most universities offer through something typically called the 'Academic Writing Support Unit'.

One danger you face is that by writing up chapter by chapter as you go along your project may get a kind of bolted-together feel to it. Once you have finished the first draft, go through the whole text making sure that this is not the case. You can achieve this by ending each chapter with a short linking paragraph, connecting that chapter to the next one. A good metaphor is that of a soap on television – each episode is 'stand alone' yet at the same time each leads seamlessly to the next one. Your linking paragraphs are almost 'teasers' encouraging the reader to see what is coming next. Overall what you write is not unlike a detective story, the slow and systematic unravelling of a mystery at the end of the narrative.

Table 10.3 gives some general tips on getting your style right.

TABLE 10.3   Some tips on writing style

The project is a formal piece of academic work, not a piece of journalism, and should therefore be written in a style that is appropriate:

- Try to avoid the first person, unless you know your supervisor approves of this form, but at the same time avoid clumsy references to 'the author" or 'the researcher'.
- Sometimes the use of the passive voice is a way to resolve the first point above: 'Information was collected' works better than 'I collected information'.
- Use the past tense – the project is an account of completed research, not an account of what you were planning to do.
- Avoid the use of nicknames or over-familiar usages: 'Beckham', not 'Becks', or God forbid 'Goldenballs'.
- Avoid 'statements' that simply reflect popular sentiment as you happen to perceive it rather than hard fact, supported by appropriate citation and reference.
- For heaven's sake get your use of the apostrophe right. 'It's' is short for 'it is' or 'it has', and is therefore an inappropriately informal form; 'its' is the equivalent of 'his' or 'her'; it follows that 'it's' is invariably wrong in a project – either it is inappropriately informal or it's bad punctuation. Note also 'one company', 'two companies' and 'the company's structure' (for example).
- Make sure you don't confuse 'there' and 'their'.
- Make good use of the spellchecker in Word – it's there for a purpose.
- Remember the Halo effect – readers (and these are predominantly the markers!) may think, even subconsciously, 'sloppy punctuation, sloppy thinking, sloppy project' as soon as they spot an error.

Getting the referencing right

We've noted before how you can make life easier for yourself when writing if you use 'cite-as-you-write' software alongside Word (see page 70). You may have noticed already that lecturers are a bit on the paranoid side about citing and referencing fully and correctly, and this is especially the case with projects. Let's have a look at why this is.

There are four very good reasons why it is necessary to reference your project:

- as research work, it is necessary to have an audit trail – the reader needs to be given directions to your sources
- to make clear which ideas are your own, by making clear which ideas you have 'borrowed', and thus to avoid accusations of plagiarism
- to allow any subsequent readers to find your original sources if they want to
- to validate claims you make.

To flag up any ideas which you have 'borrowed', you place a citation in the text – you will find them in this book in the form of '(Beech, 2013)' (without the inverted commas that is). In other words, you cite by mentioning the author of the work you are 'borrowing' from, and the year that the work first appeared. For each citation, you have a full reference in the bibliography at the end of your project. For example, this book would probably appear in the bibliography as:

Beech, J. (2015) *Doing Your Research Project,* London: Sage.

I say 'probably' because there are a number of different systems, or conventions, for how exactly you make an entry in a bibliography, and in fact how you form a citation. They all operate on the same basic principle of a series of rules, one for each form of work, such as a journal article, a book, a chapter in an edited book, a website. The system used most commonly is the Harvard system, but unfortunately this appears to be the system with the most local variations! Your university will certainly have a recommended way of citing and referencing, and you should make sure that you use it consistently throughout your project.

> Make sure you have a copy of the handout on the system of citation and referencing which your university uses. This is normally available from your university library or by downloading a copy from your university intranet (e.g. Moodle, BlackBoard).

As well as the detailed information on how to record each type of work, you will find instructions on how to structure your bibliography. A typical set is given in Table 10.4, but make sure you use your university's.

TABLE 10.4   Typical set of rules for constructing a bibliography

- Only include references for works you have actually cited, and not those you have just consulted.
- Write your bibliography as a single list at the end of your project.
- Do not produce separate bibliographies at the end of each chapter.
- Do not break your bibliography into separate lists for different types of work.
- Sort your list alphabetically by author, and chronologically where there is more than one entry for any particular author.

> The notion of 'borrowing' from a published work sometimes causes confusion. By doing Reflective Exercise 4 on page 159, make sure you are not confused.
>
> This is especially important if you come from a non-UK educational background. In different countries there are different views of what is and what isn't plagiarism. It's not a case of the UK system being 'right' and other countries 'wrong'; it's a case of you knowing what the UK standards are which you must comply with.

Do I just print it off and hand it in in the usual way?

Almost certainly not – check your university's technical specification!

You will probably have to produce two copies, and they need to be bound in a particular way.

Make sure your hand-in is exactly what your degree programme specifies for your project

Write in your answers below.

How many copies need to be handed in?

How do they need to be bound?

Do I need to add anything to it like a 'Personal declaration'?

Where do I hand it in? What is the deadline for handing it in (day and time)?

You need to check out how long it will take to have the copies bound. This can be vital as you need to match this with the hand-in deadline. Nothing can be worse after all your efforts than to find you miss the hand-in deadline because you didn't allow enough time for binding. I would also advise that you allow yourself plenty of time for printing off – university printers will be very busy with all the other projects being printed, and Word can be very unfriendly when printing longer documents.

How will I know if it's any good?

If you've worked closely with your supervisor and had him/her read through your Methodology chapter, and stuck to what you said you were going to do, you should have a pretty good idea of whether your project is good or bad.

If you can honestly answer 'yes' to all the questions in the checklist below (Table 10.5), you won't have much to worry about.

TABLE 10.5   Basic checklist for your project

Does it have a clearly stated central research question?
Is the central research question a valid *research* question?
Is the project structured in the recommended way?
Is the methodology:
- clearly stated
- logically flawless
- and actually complied with?

Are your methods rigorous, in that they are:
- sufficient
- appropriate
- justified?

Is there a good sense of narrative flow, rather than a feeling of being a series of chapters bolted together?
Are your conclusions:
- inescapable
- meaningful
- useful
- valid?

These are the basic questions that the markers will be asking. A more detailed checklist is given in Table 10.6.

TABLE 10.6   More detailed checklist for your project

Literature review	Tick if 'yes'
Have you read widely enough?	
Have you identified the theory areas that are relevant?	
Have you noted any limits on applying particular frameworks?	
Aims and objectives	
Is there a central research question that has driven your work?	
Has it been clearly stated?	
Have the aims and research objectives been clearly stated?	
Have they been used to help develop your project?	
Have they been referred to as you have written up your project?	

(Continued)

TABLE 10.6   (Continued)

Literature review	Tick if 'yes'

Methodology

Have you used an appropriate approach to answer your central research question?

Have you justified your choice of approach? Have you justified not using other approaches?

Have you correctly recognised how specific or how general the outcomes of your research will be?

Have you correctly recognised what the relevant issues and concepts are?

Analysis

Have you been rigorous in your analysis?

Does your argument flow logically from data to conclusions?

Is your reasoning clear, straightforward and correct?

Have you made appropriate comparisons?

Conclusions

Are your conclusions appropriate?

Do they relate to your stated aims and research objectives?

Do they answer your central research question?

Have you made appropriate recommendations?

Have you realised the implications of your research?

Project presentation

Have you acknowledged the sources of the theoretical frameworks?

Have you referenced all sources in the text?

Have you used a consistent and adequate referencing system?

Is your report well structured and in a natural order?

Is the abstract accurate?

Are the spelling and grammar acceptable?

Are your tables and figures correctly numbered?

You can also 'self mark' your project against the published criteria which are used in grading projects. This you should find in the project module website in your university intranet.

Handing in electronically

Very many universities require you to submit your completed project electronically through something called Turnitin. This is a vast online database which checks your project against the records it has stored and produces a 'plagiarism rating'. Depending on your individual university, you may be allowed one final submission, or you may also be allowed a dummy run beforehand.

In the latter case you may be concerned by a high rating, say one of 30 or more. This can happen in one of three ways:

1. You have plagiarised, and Turnitin has caught you.
2. You have 'accidentally plagiarised', and used other people's work without citation and referencing.
3. You have appeared to have 'accidentally plagiarised', although you have used other people's work with citation and referencing.

If it's point 1, I can't help you. If it's point 2, the remedy is in your hands – go over your text and insert the appropriate citations and references.

If it's point 3, you will not be guilty of plagiarism, but you will have produced a project that is over-dependent on other people's work, and lacks enough of your own writing. Again the remedy is in your hands – make sure there is a higher level of content which you yourself have written.

Does your project need online checking for possible plagiarism?

Check out what happens at your university.
   Does it require you to make a submission to Turnitin?
   If it does:

- find out how to do it, and
- find out how many submissions you can make.

What happens after I hand it in?

Your project will be marked by two lecturers, one of whom is your supervisor. Once they have both marked it independently, they will meet and agree a final mark. You'd be surprised how close the two marks usually are. Then again, perhaps you wouldn't, as you will have realised that in spite of the enormous variation in content, all projects are produced to a single 'template' which is defined by a common research process. Occasionally there are larger differences in marking, and these typically arise over a difference of opinion over one specific aspect of the project in question. In these cases there may be a third marking, again independently, if the two markers can't agree, and then the three markers will sit down and discuss your project until finally they reach an agreed mark.

For most of your other modules, your work will normally have been marked only once, with only a sample from your group having been second-marked by another lecturer in the department. Not only are all projects double-marked within the department, but a sample is assessed a third time by someone called the external examiner. This is someone from another university who has been appointed to quality-control all the coursework and exam scripts produced on your degree programme by second and final year students (first years' work is not normally sent to the external examiner because it normally doesn't count towards your final degree grade).

In short, your project will be the most heavily assessed piece of work you will produce throughout your course, and you can be very confident that it will have been marked accurately and fairly.

In most universities, although the project is technically 'coursework', it is treated like an exam, and you will get your mark at the time you get your full set of marks after the various assessment boards have been held. This can be frustrating for you, but it happens because of the amount of assessing that all the very long projects go through.

Most universities have a Viva (or spoken assessment, like an interview) as at least a possible requirement. In most UK universities this very rarely happens, but a number of Continental university systems include a compulsory Viva. In the UK it can happen in one of two circumstances:

- There is a suspicion of plagiarism, and you will be required to show in the Viva that you really did write what you handed in.
- The markers simply can't agree and want to find out your thoughts about your project, and so come to an agreed final mark.

Practice in other parts of Europe varies, and you should check what the procedure at your university is in theory and in practice.

I emphasise that even if this may very rarely happen at your university, should it happen to you, go and see your supervisor before the Viva takes place.

Chapter conclusion

In this chapter we have explored the issues surrounding writing up your project. Key issues are getting the right structure of content as prescribed by your university, and using the right style of English. If you have any doubts, consult your supervisor. It's not reasonable to ask him/her to read through the whole project before you submit it, but many universities specify that it is reasonable for a supervisor to be asked to read through one single chapter. If that's the case, I would suggest that you ask your supervisor to read through your completed methodology chapter – that is the one that is really the key to the rest of your project.

Section conclusion

These two chapters (Chapters 9 and 10) have taken you through the processes and practices of actually producing your project, that is, the stages that happen after the long preparation phase.

It may seem to you that this should be the end, but assuming that you haven't had to print off your first draft and immediately hand it in because you have been running so late with your work, there is time to polish your first draft, and see if you can make any late improvements. It is this that we turn to in the next (and final) chapter.

SECTION 5

Conclusion

11

Some Final Thoughts

Section and chapter guide

This final chapter, which is the only one in the final section, follows on from themes in the last two chapters by looking at how you can refine your project once you have completed the first draft.

Before we turn to that though, I suggest some further reading for you. You should have some sense of where you coasted and where you struggled while working your way through this book, so I have made recommendations relevant to specific aspects of doing your project.

The chapter concludes with some ironic (and I hope amusing) 'tips' on how to go badly wrong – in other words, don't follow these 'tips'! They are a checklist of what *not* to do.

Can you recommend any further reading?

You mean apart from those books I've already recommended in the boxes throughout the book? Well, yes there are some useful all-round books, which you can find in the box at the end of this chapter. You need to be careful in what you pick. Don't just rush into the library or the local bookshop and grab books which you have chosen by their title. At the very least, read the blurb on the back.

In choosing a book to use, consider:

- Whether it focuses on management/business research: there are a few more general research books – for example, books on research in the social sciences – which might be useful, but they may contain advice that is more appropriate for students of other subjects. My advice would be to steer clear of them.

- Whether it is aimed at an undergraduate audience: if the book is aimed at too high a level (e.g. at the PhD student), that will probably make it too complex to understand easily, and certainly too complex to understand quickly – an important point.

Above all, don't forget the most obvious resources: your notes and the recommended textbooks from the lectures you have been given!

Any last tips?

The most obvious one is always be systematic, both with your project itself, and with the way you use this book. As well as providing you with the means to produce your project, it is meant to be used as a reference book – keeping coming back and dipping into the chapters which are appropriate at that time.

Projects always go a lot more smoothly if you pay close attention to a) scheduling, b) planning and c) always having a Plan B up your sleeve. The deadline may seem a long time ahead, but the clock is ticking …

Finally it's worth considering the contents of my 'file of horrors' – examples of projects that I have come across as supervisor, second marker or external examiner at nine universities. Whatever pressures you are under, the examples in Table 11.1 can never be justified.

Table 11.1 lists some of the ways in which students have gone badly wrong during the design phase, the research phase or the writing-up phase.

TABLE 11.1   Projects gone bad!

- The student has written an extended essay rather than a project.

  This is all too easy to do if you haven't developed a rigorous methodology, and a logical flow from central research question, through aims to research objectives. Without the constraints this imposes, you can drift all too easily into a rambling commentary interspersed with your own opinions.
- The student has analysed the data gathered, but hasn't bothered to synthesise, interpret the findings or draw any conclusions.

  Doing the analysis is only the first half of the core process. Yes, you've broken down the problem into manageable parts, but without synthesis you cannot draw conclusions, and you will not have found an answer to your central research question.
- The student has rushed out and gathered the (wrong) data before sitting down and working out the appropriate methodology.

  This can arise if you are too much of an eager beaver. It's oh so tempting to gather data in the summer holiday before your final year. There is nothing wrong with that if you have rationally determined what data exactly you need to gather. Without that rationale, you end up simply gathering the most available data. It's pretty unlikely to be what you need to help answer your central research question.

- The student has rushed out and gathered all the data before deciding how to analyse it – always remember the importance of conducting a pilot or test run.

  A similar situation to the one above. In this case though, the potential problem is that you can't actually analyse the data you have gathered.

- The student has lacked the inspiration to find at least an initial topic and central research question, and has fallen back on the thankless supervisor hoping he/she will wave a magic wand.

  Remember it's your project, not your supervisor's!

- The student has ignored the supervisor's advice.

  Supervisors give advice for good reason. The worst crime is simply not listening – it never ceases to amaze me just how often a student sitting in a project supervision session is more interested in rehearsing his/her next question to put to the supervisor rather than simply listening to the answer to the question under consideration. I guess it's just anxiety, so do force yourself to listen to answers!

- The student has used a method which is inappropriate.

  Easily done, as we can see in Reflective Exercise 5 (page 150). It can arise if you make the mistake of deciding which method you are going to use as a starting point. For example, if you start by deciding you are going to use questionnaires, you may well find that questionnaires don't actually work well in answering your particular central research question. It's a bit like a mechanic deciding which tools he is going to use before he actually looks to see what the problem is with the car in for repair.

- The student hasn't bothered to explain and justify the chosen approach.

  Remember, the mark for your project is based on the written words that you handed in – you can't assume the lecturer marking it will automatically know why you chose the particular approach.

- The student has ignored the university's technical specification for the project, setting out the work in the wrong font and/or spacing, and/or getting it bound in a non-standard form.

  You risk at least having to get it rebound in the correct format, and at worst you risk having it rejected.

- The student has not related the analysis to the theoretical frameworks set out in the literature review.

  By doing this, you break that awesome logical flow you were trying to achieve.

- The student has used theoretical frameworks in the analysis that were not even mentioned in the literature review.

  Again, you break the logical flow by throwing in a new theoretical framework at the last minute.

- The student has used the wrong statistical tests.
- The student has selected a highly biased sample.
- The student has left all the work until the last minute.
  Remember, I just said the clock is ticking ...
- The study has failed to cite and reference thoroughly and consistently, using the required method.

  Citing and referencing properly isn't simply a good habit – it protects you from an accusation of plagiarism.

- The student has actually plagiarised.
  Whatever pressures you are under, this can never be justified.

Section and chapter conclusion

By the time you finally hand in your project to be assessed, you've probably got so close to it that you have lost sight of some of the things you have learned and skills you developed during the process.

As well as having learned a systematic way of doing academic research, I hope you acquired some habits which you will carry with you throughout your life. In particular, I hope you have learned:

- To question the basis of 'statements of fact' that are presented to you. Personally, I'm particularly suspicious when anyone adds to a statement the word 'fact!'. It just presses a button in me wanting to know what the evidence is to claim the statement as 'fact'.
- Always to seek evidence-based arguments to support any case you are making, especially in the context of work.

There is a concept called 'received wisdom' which refers to 'facts which are generally held to be true'. All too often even a little research would show that these 'facts' are often simply not true. Learn to be naturally questioning!

And finally ... I suppose this is the point where I should wish you 'Good Luck!'. In fact, I'm not going to, for the simple reason that producing a project has almost nothing to do with luck. I say 'almost' because there are times when luck comes into it, for example, getting access to senior staff to interview, but, by and large, producing a project is about systematic design and systematically putting that design into practice. If you can do that, you will not need any luck – you will have produced a good project.

 Recommended further reading

The best all-round books for helping you through your project (obviously as well as this one!) are:

Saunders, M. et al. (2009) *Research Methods for Business Students* (5th edn), Harlow: Pearson Education.

The 'granddaddy' of books for undergraduate business research projects. At 655 pages, there is an awful lot in there!

Collis, J. and Hussey, R. (2009) *Business Research: A Practical Guide for Undergraduate and Postgraduate Students* (3rd edn), Basingstoke: Palgrave Macmillan.

Again, a potentially useful book, but still a lot to get through at 420 pages.

Burns, R.B. (2000) *Introduction to Research Methods* (4th edn), London: Sage.

At 624 pages, I'll say no more.

Fisher, C. (2007) *Researching and Writing a Dissertation for Business Students* (2nd edn), Harlow: FT Prentice Hall.

A more manageable 376 pages.

Those of you who are thinking of proceeding to a Masters degree might wish to consider:

Bryman, A. and Bell, E. (2003) *Business Research Methods*, Oxford: Oxford University Press.

Hussey, J. and Hussey, R. (1997) *Business Research: A Practical Guide for Undergraduate and Postgraduate Students*, Basingstoke: Macmillan Business.

but if you are just wanting to stick at Bachelor these two are not for you.

If you want a lower level book, try:

Allison, B., Hilton, A., O'Sullivan, T. and Owen, A. (1996) *Research Skills for Students*, London: Kogan Page.

Oliver, P. (1997) *Teach Yourself Research for Business, Marketing and Education*, London: Hodder & Stoughton.

which are highly recommended as starter books if you are daunted by the project. Both are now a little dated, but still very good nonetheless.

The following works are also worth consulting:

Bell, J. (2005) *Doing Your Research Project: A Guide for First-Time Researchers in Education, Health and Social Science*, Buckingham: Open University Press.

Creswell, J.W. (2009) *Research Design: Qualitative, Quantitative, and Mixed Methods Approaches* (3rd edn), Thousand Oaks: Sage.

Easterby-Smith, M. et al (2012) *Management Research* (4th edn), Newbury Park: Sage.

Gill, J. and Johnson, P. (2002) *Research Methods for Managers* (3rd edn), Newbury Park: Sage.

Jankowicz, A.D. (2004) *Business Research Projects for Students* (4th edn), Andover: Thompson Learning.

Johns, N. and Lee-Ross, D. (1998) *Research Methods in Service Industry Management*, Andover: Thompson Learning.

Robson, C. (2002) *Real World Research* (2nd edn), Chichester: John Wiley & Sons.

(Continued)

(Continued)

Sharp, J.A., Peters, J. and Howard, K. (1996) *The Management of a Student Research Project* (2nd edn), Aldershot: Gower.

Veal, A.J. (2006) *Research Methods for Leisure and Tourism* (3rd edn), Harlow: FT Prentice Hall.

This is not an exhaustive list and you will find other relevant books in your library. Each has its strengths and weaknesses, and, note well, its relevance or otherwise to your specific project. Often books are aimed at particular groups of students and you should make sure you refer to one which is targeted at the right level – undergraduate/first degree – and for the right academic discipline – some are aimed, for example, at Health Services students rather than Business Studies.

Reflective Exercises to Develop Your Research Skills and Competences

For these exercises to be helpful in developing your research skills and competences, it is essential that you don't just read through them and then promptly skip to the suggested answers.

They are the book equivalent of the seminars you are used to at university. In this case you are likely to be working alone rather than in a small group. Work your way through each exercise, but only after you have written your thoughts down should you compare them with the suggested answer.

It's difficult to say how long each one will take you, but let's just say that five minutes isn't enough! Remember, the more you put into doing the exercise, the more you will get out of it.

Reflective Exercise 1

Beckham and 'a Nation's Hangover'

The following appeared on teletext, in the News section, at lunchtime on the day after the World Cup match referred to:

NATION SUFFERS IN VICTORY

England is nursing a national hangover after celebrating the sensational 1–0 World Cup victory over Argentina.

It started with the longest lunch hour in history as millions downed tools to watch the drama unfold and many failed to return to work afterwards. Jubilant fans toasted the victory and inspirational captain David Beckham, whose penalty keeps Cup hopes alive.

ITV Oracle teletext p. 312. First accessed 8 June 2002, 13:17 hrs.

Questions (write in your thoughts for each answer):

1. Is this 'News'? Is each of the statements 'fact' or someone's personal 'impression'?

2. What can be inferred from the lack of any mention of how the 'evidence' quoted was actually gathered?

3. To give academic rigour to each of the statements made, what research would have to have been undertaken?

4. What sort of sample and sample size do think would be necessary to make statements about the population of England?

5. Do you think it would have been possible to have undertaken such research in the given timeframe?

6. What mistake has the anonymous author made?

Once you have written your thoughts, and only then, turn to page 152 and review the suggested answers.

Reflective Exercise 2

Reviewing Potential Central Research Questions

Consider the following central research questions:

1. What does the future hold for English football with respect to satellite broadcasting?

2. What was the reasoning behind Jaguar's decision to re-enter Formula 1 motor racing?

3. How has North Korea differentiated its sports venues?

4. Is motivation important in the management of bar workers?

5. Do men and women behave differently in the way they use the internet?

6. Why do spectators attend [insert the name of a local professional sports club which plays in a league] home games and what are the factors that attract them to attend or dissuade them from attending?

7. What do visitors to museums buy as presents to take home?

8. Is there a need for a standard code of ethics at leisure centres?

Questions (write in your thoughts as to each answer)

For each of the above central research questions, consider the following:

1. What, if anything, is wrong with these central research questions for a research project?

2. How might each one be 'tweaked' to become acceptable CRQs?

Once you have written your thoughts below to each central research question, and only then, turn to page 154 and review the suggested answers.

Reflective Exercise 3

Bias in Your Data

Imagine you decide to collect data from the general public through the use of question-naires. One Thursday morning, you position yourself on your local High Street and ask passers-by to fill in your questionnaire.

In what ways would your sample tend to be biased? Which segments of the general public would be likely to be over-represented and under-represented?

Write in your suggestions below.

Once you have written your thoughts, and only then, turn to page 157 and review the suggested answers.

Reflective Exercise 4

What Is and Isn't Plagiarism

Listed below are six variations of 'borrowing' from the published work of an author.

They vary from number 1, which all would agree is definitely plagiarism, through to number 6, which all would agree is not plagiarism. It follows that at some point as we move down the list, we cross from 'plagiarism' to 'not plagiarism'.

Where do you draw the line between the two? Think long and hard and then write in where you draw the line, for example between number 2 and number 3.

Note: For this exercise, a bibliography is defined as a list of books relevant to the piece of writing but not necessarily cited in the text; a reference list contains all the sources cited in the text.

1. Copying a paragraph word for word from a source without any acknowledgement.

2. Copying a paragraph and making small changes – e.g. replacing a few words with similar meaning words, but without giving a citation, including the source in the bibliography.

3. Cutting and pasting a paragraph by using sentences of the original but omitting one or two and putting one or two in a different order, no quotation marks; in-text acknowledgement, e.g. (Jones, 1999), plus inclusion in the bibliography.

4. Composing a paragraph by taking short phrases of ten to fifteen words from a number of sources and putting them together, adding words of your own to make a coherent whole; all sources included in the bibliography.

5. Paraphrasing a paragraph with substantial changes in language and organisation; the new version will also have changes in the amount of detail used and the examples cited; in-text acknowledgement, e.g. (Jones, 1999), and inclusion in the bibliography.

6. Quoting a paragraph by placing it in block format with the source both cited in the text and listed in the bibliography.

Draw a line across the page to show where you think we change from 'plagiarism' to 'not plagiarism'. Then, and only then, turn to page 159.

Based on an exercise in Swales and Feak (1993).

Reflective Exercise 5 – The Suit that Makes You Feel Old

 NEWS

A suit that simulates old age is helping architects design more user-friendly hospitals

The Third Age Suit restricts the mobility of the wearer to give them an appreciation of what it is like for patients getting around the hospital.

Architects from Capita Symonds are using the suit to help them redesign the Derby City General Hospital.

The suit was developed by scientists at Loughborough University and adapted by the building firm Skanska.

It was first designed in conjunction with Ford, which used it to test the design of the Ford Focus car for healthy elderly people.

Restricted movement

Skanska and the Trust have modified this to have an insight into the problems that patients with reduced mobility might have in hospitals.

This reduced mobility could be due to clinical conditions like arthritis and multiple sclerosis or recovering from surgery or an accident and can affect young as well as old people.

The suit has splints and restrictors that limit the movement of joints such as the hand, wrists, elbows, neck, upper and lower torso, knees and ankles to simulate the loss of mobility caused by ageing and arthritis.

Yellow goggles mimic the declining vision, increased sensitivity to glare and reduced sensitivity to blue light experienced by many people as they age.

Surgical style gloves are also provided to mimic the reduction in tactile sensitivity that occurs as a result of changes in the skin and sensory receptors.

The architects found the simplest of tasks, such as sitting down, standing up and reaching out the arm, became laboured and difficult when wearing the suit.

They identified getting through doors, accessing patient wardrobes and reaching towels as potential problems and have already reviewed their proposed designs for the hospital.

Howard Jeffrey, design manager for Skanska, said: 'It was fantastic how immediate the discussion was. As soon as they had put the suit on they recognised what was not going to work in their design and changed it.

'As a contractor, we can now change the designs at no extra cost.'

He said nurses and people in the hospitals could also get an insight into what patients experience by wearing the suit.

Brian Ibell from Derby Hospitals NHS Trust said: 'With the increasing ageing population we need to understand more about mobility problems encountered by patients and how we can design more appropriate facilities.

'This piece of research is a step forward for designers working on any hospital scheme and will certainly benefit Derby Hospitals.'

A spokeswoman from Help the Aged said: 'It's a fantastic idea.

'To really experience say visual or hearing loss you have got to take away that sense. It's that same type of theory here.

'To actually understand what it's like to be without mobility you have to take it away.

'The awareness both for practitioners and everybody of how difficult it can be to live with reduced mobility is real progress.'

She said although the majority of us will suffer some loss of mobility as we get older there are ways to prevent it, such as exercise and good nutrition.

Story from BBC NEWS: http://news.bbc.co.uk/go/pr/fr/-/1/hi/health/3538220.stm Published: 2004/08/05 13:29:41 GMT © BBC MMIV (www.bbc.co.uk/foi/about/copyright.shtml)

Questions

1. To what extent would the results of these simulations be valid?

2. Are there more appropriate research methods that could be used?

Once you have written your thoughts, and only then, turn to page 160 and review the suggested answers.

Reflective Exercise 1 – Beckham and 'a Nation's Hangover'

1. Is this 'News'? Is each of the statements 'fact' or someone's personal 'impression'?

No it's not! The 'statements' are someone's personal impression – generalising from the specific, probably shaped by the fact that the author was nursing a hangover but had to meet a news deadline.

2. What can be inferred from the lack of any mention of how the 'evidence' quoted was actually gathered?

There is no evidence base for his claims. I'm assuming from the laddish nature of the report that the author was male, although I would have to admit there is no evidence to confirm this view!

3. To give academic rigour to each of the statements made, what research would have to have been undertaken?

The author should have taken the views of a representative and unbiased sample, rather than just sampled his mates.

4. What sort of sample and sample size would be necessary to make statements about the population of England?

A sample would have to have been constructed to reflect age, sex, ethnicity and socio-economic distribution of the whole population. It is worth noting that in general election opinion polls the samples taken are about 2,000 people in size.

5. Do you think it would have been possible to have undertaken such research in the given timeframe?

Clearly not.

6. What mistake has the anonymous author made?

He has assumed that his personal experience was representative of the population.

To show how wrong he was in making this assumption, just consider the number of people who fall into categories such as the household of the author of this book – his wife and his then 81-year-old mother-in-law have absolutely no interest in football; he supports Scotland and might well have celebrated if Argentina had won; none of his numerous grandchildren are old enough to suffer from hangovers. The Teletext author assumes that the entire population consists of 18–30-year-old alpha males and ladettes.

What you should have learned by doing this exercise

- In research, your argument is only as strong as the evidence you have to support it.
- To represent the views of a 'population' you must have a sample which is accurately representative.
- Skewed or biased samples will give misleading results – either review your sample or redefine your population so that your sample is representative.
- You need to think about the size of your sample – is it big enough to give you 95 per cent confidence in the results for the size of population you are researching? Note that to do this you will need to know the size of your population.
- Beware of generalising from the specific.

Reflective Exercise 2 – Reviewing Potential Central Research Questions

1. What does the future hold for English football with respect to satellite broadcasting?

If you could see the future, you would be walking on water, not studying at university! This is not a research question – it leads to speculation, which may well be informed speculation (reasonable as an essay) but does not lead to a logical and irrefutable answer (required for a project). The topic is OK, it's just the CRQ that is the problem. Lots of good CRQs are possible.

As it's phrased, this will turn out as little more than sheer speculation. It's the kind of question that the more serious journalist loves to have a crack at. The topic is an interesting one, but to produce a good CRQ, it's back to the drawing board I'm afraid.

2. What was the reasoning behind Jaguar's decision to re-enter Formula 1 motor racing?

The problem here is that the answer to the question is not unknown; at least the Jaguar directors know the answer. The only gap in knowledge is a gap in public knowledge. Answering it is a matter of investigative journalism, not of academic research. If it were a suitable research question, another issue would be the appropriate methodology – ask the Jaguar directors. The reality is that they would not be prepared to discuss commercially confidential matters of strategy with an undergraduate student. The topic is OK, it's just the CRQ that is the problem. Generally a difficult area if you are dependent on access to industry data which will not be made available to you.

Like the first one, it's a topic with potential. There are certainly plenty of appropriate theoretical frameworks from strategy that can be applied for your analysis.

3. How has North Korea differentiated its sports venues?

Great question in fact! The problem is that it is simply unanswerable by someone studying in the EU. Perhaps the ultimate access problem – I'm assuming, of course, that your uncle isn't the head of the North Korea tourist board. Not only would it be impossible to get secondary data, it would also be impossible to get primary data. The data you need is not available on the internet, the authorities in North Korea are uncooperative, and you wouldn't get a visa even if you were prepared to go to North Korea. Great idea, but forget it as downright unworkable, both as a CRQ and a topic. Oh, and have you considered the possibility that they don't in fact differentiate them, or even want to differentiate them!

In this case, even the topic, with respect to North Korea, is unworkable. That's the part that needs tweaking to a country which is 'doable'.

4. Is motivation important in the management of bar workers?

The trouble with this one is that it doesn't need a 10,000 word research project to provide an answer – we know the answer is 'Yes'! The CRQ could be sharpened into something worthwhile by being more specific. A good topic none the less, and one where you might well have good access because of your part-time work experience.

It's the question word which is the problem – choosing a plain yes/no question doesn't make sense.

5. Do men and women behave differently in the way they use the internet?

Using the internet for online shopping would qualify as an appropriate topic for a business project, but the more general question posed here of how people use the internet goes way beyond being appropriate as a business topic.

So, by adding 'for online shopping' to the CRQ we would make it appropriate. The problem is that it would then cover an enormous area, much too big for an undergraduate business project. To make it workable, you could 'close it down' by looking at a specified demographic sector, for example, students, or a specified retail sector.

6. Why do spectators attend [insert the name of a local professional sports club which plays in a league] home games and what are the factors that attract them to attend or dissuade them from attending?

The most obvious problem is that this isn't a CRQ – it's two CRQs! And two very similar ones at that. They are slightly different in that the second one covers negative as well as positive factors. Cutting half the present attempt out and a bit of tweaking could produce a good CRQ.

7. What do visitors to museums buy as presents to take home?

Even if your degree programme is Tourism Management, you might be surprised to learn that there is one big gap here, just waiting for undergraduate contributions! So, on the face of it, a good CRQ. But get real – you would have to set some limits, such as a particular type of museum (e.g. industrial heritage), a type of souvenir (e.g. ornaments that identify

(Continued)

(Continued)

the destination), and/or an identified visitor-generating area (e.g. tourists from Japan). You'd need to think about access too – how would you track down, for example, 50 tourists who would be willing to fill in questionnaires? There might be a seasonality issue too.

8. Is there a need for a standard code of ethics at leisure centres?

Shades of number 4 here! I'm tempted to say the answer is 'Yes!', not 10,000 words.

Is it a CRQ for tweaking then? Well, I have some reservations, in particular that, as it stands, it's not clearly embedded in business and management as topics go. You might just get away with it if you spun it into marketing and customer care, or an analysis of whether health spas are actually meeting customer needs. It would be workable if it was tweaked into an investigation of what exactly clients have ethical concerns about. It would be interesting to establish whether different segments of leisure centre users have different concerns. Realistically it would be sensible to restrict the investigation to a specific small geographical area. The number within that area would influence your methodology (see page 87).

The whole health and lifestyle sector is growing in terms of the interest shown by researchers. Still plenty of gaps to be filled.

By the way, if you were expecting eight finely crafted ready-to-go CRQs to appear on this page, I can only disappoint you! After all, as I said above, the inspiration must come from you. In any case, I've made these eight up, and obviously have not tested whether in practice they would work even if tweaked. So don't use them as a blueprint – come up with your own ideas, with topics that actually interest you. In any case, once the first student had ripped off one of my CRQs there wouldn't actually be a gap in knowledge, would there?

Reflective Exercise 3 – Bias in Your Data

Let's first consider the sections of the general public who might be over-represented.

1. Thursday is 'pension day', so you will probably have an over-representation of people aged over 65.

2. They would be retired, in other words, not employed.

3. Most employed people would be at their work rather than walking in the High Street.

4. As it's a High Street there would be an over-representation of town dwellers.

5. There would be an over-representation of homemakers, which might mean an over-representation of females.

6. If you are in a town or city which has a university in it, the 18–21-year-olds might be over-represented.

7. There might be visitors from other places in your sample, giving an over-representation of non-residents' views.

By definition, the following would be likely to be under-represented (match each group with the group above with the same number):

1. There would be an under-representation of people aged under 65.

2. There would be an under-representation of people who are employed.

3. There would an even greater under-representation of people who are employed.

4. There would be an under-representation of country-dwellers.

5. There would be an under-representation of 'sole breadwinners', which might mean an under-representation of males.

(Continued)

(Continued)

6. If you are in a town or city which has a university in it, the over-21-year-olds might be under-represented.

7. There might be visitors from other places in your sample, giving an under-representation of residents' views.

The pair numbered 7 would be a problem if you have defined your topic in terms of the town or city where you are gathering data.

Reflective Exercise 4 – What Is and Isn't Plagiarism

Well, where did you draw the line?

UK lecturers would normally draw the line between number 4 and number 5. If that's where you drew the line, you can relax – your idea of plagiarism is the same as the people who will be assessing your project.

If you drew the line higher up, between number 2 and number 3 for example, there is a definite problem – the people assessing your project do not share your rather relaxed view, and may well accuse you of plagiarism to your surprise. It's not a case of who is right and who is wrong; it's a question of you recognising the UK standard by which you will be judged. You will need to adopt a much stricter view of citation and referencing if you want to keep out of trouble.

If you drew the line between number 5 and number 6 you can definitely relax – your view is actually stricter than is necessary.

Reflective Exercise 5 – The Suit that Makes You Feel Old

1. To what extent would the results of these simulations be valid?

There are two problems with this research design which would tend to produce invalid data.

Firstly, the subjects are young people and hence think in a young way. Their ingenuity and persistence might be quite different from that of old people.

Secondly, the results will be for people who are temporarily disabled – their behaviour is very likely to be different from that of people who are permanently disabled, who will have developed, at least to some extent, coping strategies. Anyone who has been temporarily confined to a wheelchair, as a result of a broken leg, for example, will have been amazed at a) how difficult, for example, negotiating swing doors is, and yet on the other hand b) how skilled permanently disabled people are in manoeuvring their wheelchairs.

2. Are there more appropriate research methods that could be used?

The whole idea of using simulation seems to me to be entirely inappropriate. Much more appropriate methods would involve the old people themselves. Best of all, one would use structured observation of old people in hospitals. If for any reason this proved problematic, one could talk to them, so focus groups or semi-structured interviews would be a fall-back alternative – not quite as valid, as people may not be 100 per cent accurate in describing their own activity.

It seems to me that using mobility restriction devices in a simulation is a classic example of 'a method in search of a methodology'. The research design was started from the wrong end – the research question should lead to an appropriate research method, not the research method go looking for a research question.

Appendix

Contact Log with your Supervisor

You are strongly advised to keep this log of contact with your supervisor. It is not implied that ten meetings are the norm; ten would be unusual and excessive even though in some circumstances ten might be necessary! In the outcome column, you should note any decisions reached and any specific targets for you to accomplish before your next meeting.

Keep this log until you receive your mark, i.e. after any possibility of being asked to attend a Viva.

Meeting	Date	Time	Duration	Specific purpose	Outcome
1					
2					
3					
4					
5					
6					
7					
8					
9					
10					

Glossary

Aims: In the context of your research project, an aim is a middle-level member of the research design hierarchy. Aims are derived from the central research question, and lead on to research objectives. See page 75.

Analyse: In the context of your research project, to analyse is to break down a problem systematically in order to understand it better.

Analytical tool: A device which can be used to help you analyse a situation. Unlike a theoretical framework, it may lack rigorous testing based on evidence.

Bias: see Input bias

Central research question (CRQ): The one overall question that encapsulates what you are trying to find out by doing your research.

Confidence interval: A measure of the accuracy of a survey, normally expressed as a plus-or-minus figure. See page 85.

Confidence level: An estimate of how well the sample taken in a survey actually reflects the whole population. By convention, researchers normally seek a 95 per cent confidence level. See page 85.

Contribution: In this context, 'contribution' refers to a contribution to the body of knowledge, in other words, a new piece of knowledge (normally quite a small one) which is the outcome of research.

Data: Systematically gathered bits of information. 'Data' is actually the plural of 'datum', but most people don't use the word 'datum' any more.

Deskwork: Conducting the gathering of secondary data. This can be conducted either at a desk in the office, using internet resources, or in a library, using good old books and journals. See also 'Fieldwork'.

Epistemology: The study of knowledge. A good detailed explanation can be found at http://plato.stanford.edu/entries/epistemology/.

Ethics: The principles of what is right and what is wrong.

Fieldwork: The gathering of primary data. This cannot be achieved by sitting in your office space or in a library, so to gather primary data you have to go out 'into the field', meaning into the organisation(s) you are researching. See also 'Deskwork'.

Functional fixedness: Seeing a management issue from the perspective of one management function (e.g. marketing, HRM or finance) only. In other words, marketing people tend to see any management problem as a marketing problem and then look for marketing solutions.

Gap (in the body of knowledge): Something which nobody knows (yet!).

Hermeneutic: see Phenomenological

Input bias: Bias which arises from the way you made your choice when sampling was inadvertently non-random.

Interpretivist: see Phenomenological

Iterative: An iterative process is one which reaches its intended goal through repetition, typically by finding better and better approximations. See Figure 1.1.

Literature review: A systematic and critical account of academic research which has already been published. See Chapter 6.

Methodology: The systematic overall design of your research.

Methods: The research tools that are used to gather your data, such as questionnaires or interviews.

Objectives: In this context, 'research objective' as opposed to 'personal objective'. The lowest and most specific layer of the research design hierarchy, research objectives are derived from aims. See page 75.

Paradigm: A consistent set of thoughts and practices which together may be seen as a way of viewing the world. Scientists, for example, talk of Einstein overthrowing the older Newtonian paradigm when he produced his Theory of Relativity. There are two major research paradigms – positivist and phenomenological.

Phenomenological: 'Phenomenological' is, for our purposes, a word used as a label for the word-based, qualitative, arts-oriented research paradigm.

Plagiarism: The passing off of someone else's work as your own, either deliberately and wilfully (a form of cheating), or accidentally, through failure to cite and reference properly.

Population: The total number in the group you are researching.

Positivist: 'Positivist' is, for our purposes, a word used as a label for the number-based, quantitative, science-oriented research paradigm.

Process: A systematic series of actions carried out in a particular order to achieve an ultimate goal.

Project: A self-contained piece of work. Throughout this book the word is used in the specific context of an undergraduate research project.

Qualitative: Pertaining to words. Qualitative data is often referred to as 'soft data'. Qualitative research is more appropriate in researching complex situations which are unlikely to produce precise solutions.

Quantitative: Pertaining to numbers. Quantitative data is often referred to as 'hard data'. Quantitative research is more appropriate in researching straightforward situations which are likely to produce precise solutions.

Quota sampling: Choosing who or what makes up your sample so that in total they reflect the population. For example, if half the population is female, then you construct a sample which is 50 per cent female.

Random sampling: The process of identifying specifically who or what will constitute your sample by choosing them randomly.

References: The references which you include at the end of your research project is a list of books, journal articles, websites, etc., which are cited in the main text. It does not include resources which you consulted but have not cited.

Reliability: The extent to which you would get the same data if you carried on repeating your data-gathering.

Research: A systematic process for adding to the body of knowledge through an evidence-based approach.

Sample: The group within the population you are measuring, from which you actually gather data.

Synthesise: In the context of your research project, to synthesise is to build up answers systematically to research questions once analysis has been conducted.

Theoretical framework: An evidence-based framework, tried and tested by an academic, which can be applied in other circumstances.

Topic: The topic of your research project is the context (in particular, the industry sector and the business function, such as marketing or finance) in which it is embedded.

Validity: The extent to which your data actually reflects the real world you are trying to measure.

References

Allard-Poesi, F. and Maréchal, C. (2001) 'Constructing the Research Problem', in R.-A. Thietart et al., *Doing Management Research*, London: Sage.

Allison, B., Hilton, A., O'Sullivan, T. and Owen, A. (1996) *Research Skills for Students*, London: Kogan Page.

Ashby, E. (1961) 'Universities Today and Tomorrow', *The Listener*, Issue 1, July.

Bell, J. (2005) *Doing Your Research Project: A Guide for First-Time Researchers in Education, Health and Social Science*, Buckingham: Open University Press.

Bloom, B.S., Engelhart, M.D., Furst, E.J., Hill, W.H. and Krathwohl, D.R. (1956) *Taxonomy of Educational Objectives: The Classification of Educational Goals. Handbook I*, New York: David McKay Publishers.

Bourqe, L. and Fielder, E.P. (2002) *How to Conduct Self-Administered and Mail Survey*s (2nd edn), London: Sage.

Bryman, A. and Bell, E. (2003) *Business Research Methods*, Oxford: Oxford University Press.

Burns, R.B. (2000) *Introduction to Research Methods* (4th edn), London: Sage.

Cassell, C. and Symon, S. (2004) *Essential Guide to Qualitative Methods in Organizational Research*, London: Sage.

Chatham House (2014) *Chatham House Rule* (online). Available at: www.chathamhouse.org/about/chatham-house-rule (last accessed 18 February 2014).

Collis, J. and Hussey, R. (2009) *Business Research: A Practical Guide for Undergraduate and Postgraduate Students* (3rd edn), Basingstoke: Palgrave Macmillan.

Creswell, J.W. (2009) *Research Design: Qualitative, Quantitative, and Mixed Methods Approaches* (3rd edn), Thousand Oaks: Sage.

de Nahlik, C. and Marshall, I. (2009) 'The Research Ethics Pentagon of Practice: Using a Schema to Deliver the Ethics Message to All Students Engaged in Research Projects', in *Proceedings of the Coventry University Faculty of Business, Environment and Society Internal Applied Research Conference*, 3 July, Coventry.

Diamantopoulos, A. and Schlegelmilch, B.B. (1997) *Taking the Fear out of Data Analysis*, London: Thompson Learning.

di Gregorio, S. (1996) 'Cranfield University PhD Research Methodology Course Notes', Cranfield, unpublished.

Easterby-Smith, M., Thorpe, R. and Jackson, P. (2012) *Management Research* (4th edn), Newbury Park: Sage.

Fink, A. (2003) *How to Manage, Analyze, and Interpret Survey Data* (2nd edn), Thousand Oaks: Sage.

Fink, A. (2008) *How to Conduct Surveys* (4th edn), Newbury Park: Sage.

Fisher, C. (2007) *Researching and Writing a Dissertation for Business Students* (2nd edn), Harlow: FT PrenticeHall.

Foddy, W. (1994) *Constructing Questions for Interviews and Questionnaires*, Cambridge: Cambridge University Press.

Gill, J. and Johnson, P. (2002) *Research Methods for Managers* (3rd edn), Newbury Park: Sage.

Gummesson, E.G. (2000) *Qualitative Methods in Management Research* (2nd edn), Thousand Oaks: Sage.

Harris, R. and Spinks, A. (2007) *The C.A.R.S. Checklist for Evaluating Internet Sources.* Available at: www.andyspinks.com/researchhelp/web/CARS.pdf (last accessed 19 February 2013).

Hart, C. (1998) *Doing a Literature Review*, Thousand Oaks: Sage.

Hussey, J. and Hussey, R. (1997) *Business Research: A Practical Guide for Undergraduate and Postgraduate Students*, Basingstoke: Macmillan Business.

Jankowicz, A.D. (2004) *Business Research Projects for Students* (4th edn), Andover: Thompson Learning.

Johns, N. and Lee-Ross, D. (1998) *Research Methods in Service Industry Management*, Andover: Thompson Learning.

Kvale, S. (2008) *Doing Interviews*, London: Sage.

Lehrer, T. (1990) 'Bright College Days' from *An Evening Wasted With Tom Lehrer*; released by Reprise/WEA as an audio CD.

Machi, L.A. and McEvoy, B.T. (2009) *The Literature Review*, Thousand Oaks: Corwin.

Maykut, P. and Morehouse, R. (1994) *Beginning Qualitative Research*, London: Falmer.

Oliver, P. (1997) *Teach Yourself Research for Business, Marketing and Education*, London: Hodder & Stoughton.

Oppenheim, A.N. (2000) *Questionnaire Design, Interviewing and Attitude Measurement*, London: Continuum.

Ornstein, M. (2013) *A Companion to Survey Research*, London: Sage.

Quality Assurance Agency for Higher Education (2007) *Subject Benchmark Statements: General Business and Management 2007*, London: QAA. Available at: www.qaa.ac.uk/Publications/InformationAndGuidance/Documents/GeneralBusinessManagement.pdf (last accessed 19 February 2013).

Remenyi, D. (2012) *Case Study Research (The Quick Guide)*, Sonning Common: Academic Publishing International.

Remenyi, D., Onofrei, G. and English, J. (2009) *An Introduction to Statistics Using Microsoft Excel*, Reading: Academic Publishing International.

Ridley, D. (2012) *The Literature Review: A Step-by-Step Guide for Students* (2nd edn), London: Sage.

Robson, C. (2002) *Real World Research* (2nd edn), Chichester: John Wiley & Sons.

Royer, I. and Zarlowski, P. (2001) 'Sampling' in R.-A. Thietart et al., *Doing Management Research*, London: Sage.

Rubin, H.J. and Rubin, I.S. (2012) *Qualitative Interviewing*, London: Sage.

Salkind, Neil J. (2010) *Statistics for People Who (Think They) Hate Statistics* (4th edn), Thousand Oaks: Sage.

Saunders, M., Thornhill, A. and Lewis, P. (2009) *Research Methods for Business Students* (5th edn), Harlow: Pearson Education.

Sharp, J.A., Peters, J. and Howard, K. (1996) *The Management of a Student Research Project* (2nd edn), Aldershot: Gower.

Swales, J.M. and Feak, C.B. (1993) *Academic Writing for Graduate Students*, Ann Arbor: University of Michigan Press.

Thietart, R.-A. et al., *Doing Management Research*, London: Sage.

Veal, A.J. (2006) *Research Methods for Leisure and Tourism* (3rd edn), Harlow: FT Prentice Hall.

Yin, R.K. (2008) *Case Study Research: Design and Methods* (4th edn), London: Sage.

Index

Tables and Figures are indicated by page numbers in bold.